CAPACITY PLANNING
FOR
COMPUTER SYSTEMS

CAPACITY PLANNING FOR COMPUTER SYSTEMS

Tim Browning

AP PROFESSIONAL

Boston   San Diego   New York
London   Sydney   Tokyo   Toronto

Copyright © 1995 by Academic Press, Inc.
All rights reserved.
No part of this publication may be reproduced or
transmitted in any form or by any means, electronic
or mechanical, including photocopy, recording, or
any information storage and retrieval system, without
permission in writing from the publisher.

All brand names and product names mentioned in this book are
trademarks or registered trademarks of their respective companies.

Chapter 7 ("Capacity Planning for IBM MVS Data Storage Systems")
is adapted from "Capacity Planning Overview," Tim Browning,
1994 Computer System Series: Peripherals, McGraw-Hill, Inc.,
Datapro Information Services, Delran, New Jersey.

AP PROFESSIONAL
955 Massachusetts Avenue, Cambridge, MA 02139

An Imprint of ACADEMIC PRESS, INC.
A Division of HARCOURT BRACE & COMPANY

United Kingdom Edition published by
ACADEMIC PRESS LIMITED
24–28 Oval Road, London NW1 7DX

Library of Congress Cataloging-in-Publication Data
Browning, Tim.
    Capacity planning for computer systems. / Tim Browning.
        p.   cm.
    Includes bibliographical references and index.
    ISBN 0-12-136490-9   (acid-free paper)
    1. Computer capacity--Planning.   I. Title.
QA76.9.C63B76 1994
004.2'068'4--dc20   94-32559
                                                     CIP

Printed in the United States of America
94 95 96 97 98 IP 9 8 7 6 5 4 3 2 1

Contents

Acknowledgments

Writing a book is not easy—especially for people in the author's environment. They probably grow weary of hearing about the book that's going to be written and it gets even worse when the writing finally starts. Then everyone wants to know when you are going to finish your book!

I wish to give special thanks to the many friends, relatives, and coworkers who have encouraged and supported me, not only for their interest, but mostly for their patience and understanding.

I am grateful for the encouragement and support from many of my colleagues at IBM and ISSC. Special thanks to Linda Pierce at ISSC—a very supportive and caring technical manager who encourages me to achieve excellence in my work.

I would like to thank Frank Schipani of Emory University and Patti Perry of ISSC, who read parts of the book and provided valuable comments. Thanks also to Bill White of ISSC for spirited philosophical discussions regarding topics in the book and to the late Ted Hughes of Equifax who suggested many of the systems management topics. A very special thanks goes to Gene Trautman, formerly of Contel, who challenged me to improve my writing ability.

I wish to thank Alan Rose, my publisher, who encouraged me to persist in my writing despite the volatility of corporate employment, personal upheavals, and sudden surprises within the publishing community.

Many thanks to all of the people at AP PROFESSIONAL and Intertext Publications who contributed to the production of this book.

I also wish to thank Heloese Bennett, who taught me the value of planning for the future while living in the present.

Particular thanks go to my partner, Dr. Daniel Trussell, for his enthusiasm and untiring support, and to our Irish Wolfhound dogs, Alexander and Ariel, who remained constant companions during the long hours spent writing this book.

Preface

Once upon a time I went into a bookstore to buy a book on capacity planning. I couldn't find one. So, I went to other bookstores. I still couldn't find one. Out of this frustration, I decided to write a book on capacity planning for computer systems. Also, like most people who buy books on technical subjects, I needed one to use in my work.

It seems that many people are involved in capacity planning activities or write papers on this subject. There are a tremendous number of technical papers and brief technical studies published in the proceedings of many technical conferences. Over the years, I have acquired some considerable experience doing capacity planning in a variety of contexts and for a variety of computer systems and networks. My objective was to have the kind of book I would want to use in my work, both as a reference book or inventory of capacity planning concepts, as well as a coherent methodology that would be well suited to the treatment of capacity planning problems for any computer system environment.

This book is planned to give the widest possible overview of the art and science of capacity planning to the widest possible audience. As such, the subjects chosen for discussion are those aspects of capacity planning that are broadly applicable . . . those that will be of interest and hopefully of benefit to individuals involved with all computer systems disciplines, backgrounds, or ambition. Because capacity planning emerged from the management of mainframe systems during the past 20 years, many of the examples used to demonstrate the concepts of capacity planning arise out of the mainframe context. Nevertheless, like many other systems management disciplines, the methodologies and concepts have application to a variety of contexts.

Is this just another legacy mainframe book? Is this another client/server or distributed systems book? The subject matter of capacity planning spans all architecture and platforms. Its principles have evolved from the works of many contributors from a variety of contexts. In these pages, we shall be blending the mathematical, statistical, and computer science bases of capacity planning with the qualitative, deductive, metaphysical, and unique capabilities normally associated with the philosophy of science. This emphasis on a systems approach to capacity planning, on a conjoining of quantitative and qualitative dimensions, reflects the activity of capacity planning itself.

This book is intended primarily for people who have some background in statistics and computer systems management and who need to perform, implement, direct, or manage capacity planning activities. Chapters are organized as much for reference as for straight-through reading.

Most capacity planning articles describe certain aspects of this discipline *in isolation*, without providing a framework to tie them together. They may tell you *how* to do things without ever telling you why you want to do them. Conversely, you may be lectured by capacity planners as to the why of doing certain things without information on how to do them. Hopefully, this is where this books fits in. While I can't claim that *everything* you need to know is included, I can guarantee that after reading it you will know pretty much what capacity planning involves and how to go about it.

Chapter 1 explores the conceptual foundations of capacity planning. This is where you will find definitions and how capacity planning is viewed within the broader contexts of business planning. Also, the differences between capacity planning, capacity management, performance management, and business planning are examined. The critical functions of capacity planning are explored—including the technical, business, and management factors brought to bear on the problem of prediction and forecasting.

Chapter 2 covers the metrics of capacity planning. Included here are the concepts and analytical structures for defining, measuring, and projecting computer systems resources. Such concepts as utilization, throughput, workload characterization, and system capacity are explored. Mathematical models for curve fitting are developed.

Chapter 3 begins with a look at the methodology of natural unit forecasting. The challenge explored here is that of relating the business activity in the enterprise served by the information systems organization to the demand for computer resources. The use of statistical analysis and modeling is explored as well as the requirements for model validation. It is also here, in the context of relating computer systems to business activity, that service levels, service goals, service-level agreements, and chargeback cost accounting are discussed in depth.

Chapter 4 is brief but is highly focused on the process of forecasting within a planning and management context. Statistical forecasting is compared to planning. Is the future a destiny, inexorably predetermined by past patterns, or is the future created by the planning process itself? How are probability and risk determined with respect to planning? What is the role of the capacity planner in predicting future resource needs? How are forecasts evaluated and communicated?

Our questions in Chapter 4 lead us to Chapter 5, a review of statistical forecasting techniques. How are causal models and time-series models used in capacity planning? What are the strengths and weaknesses of statistical forecasting? How can we represent a model in which the recent past has more influence on the future than the distant past? Finally, how should we monitor and revise our forecasts?

Chapter 6 examines an interesting case study for determining the *logical* capacity of a system as compared to the traditional *physical* capacity problem. The tools of capacity planning—statistical analysis techniques—are applied to the areas of systems optimization and queuing structures more often associated with performance management.

Chapter 7 provides an overview of the capacity planning techniques used for data storage resources such as disk and tape. Examples are taken from the MVS (IBM) systems environments. A discussion of new directions in technology, such as RAID and automated tape libraries, explores the emerging directions for both technology and systems management of data.

Chapter 8 provides an overview and set of guidelines for charting as well as graphics presentations for capacity planning. How are patterns and relationships in computer resource usage revealed using graphs? How should data be annotated? How are multiple sets of data combined? When do you use bar charts versus line charts or pie charts? What kinds of charts are specifically used in capacity planning or service-level administration? Finally, we examine the relationships between objects, symbols, and information within the graphics context and how graphics help summarize complex system relationships.

The last chapter, Chapter 9, looks at the capacity planning function within the context of systems administration and discusses the future of capacity planning. Specifically, issues of emerging technologies, such as distributed systems and client/server, are explored. What is the relationship between capacity planning and other management control disciplines? What kind of modeling or planning techniques should be used for client/server systems? How will measurements be acquired for the distributed server model to enable capacity management as an effective systems management discipline?

An appendix, which gives a brief summary of software used for capacity planning, is provided. Included are the name, company address and telephone number, type of system required (hardware and operating system), price, and a brief description. Computer operating systems covered include MVS, VM, UNIX, DEC/VAX, VMS, HP, OS/2, Windows, Windows NT, NeXT, SunOS, Apollo, HP-UX, RISC/ULTRIX, Convexos, IRIX, AIX, DG/UX, DOS/VSE, MS-DOS, PC/DOS, and DOMAIN/OS. Some of the special terminology used in this book, as well as in capacity planning in general, is listed in the glossary. The glossary is an informal and brief reminder of the major concepts and ideas central to the activity of capacity planning.

1

Capacity Planning Foundations

Good judgment comes from experience.
Experience comes from bad judgment.

— Anon.

1.1 WHAT IS CAPACITY PLANNING?

Capacity planning for computing systems arose out of the need to support critical mainframe computing and networking. Like many system management disciplines, capacity planning uses principles and methodologies that are broadly applicable to many types of resource planning needs. Encompassing a broad scope of activities, it includes most of the data and tools used in performance management, as well as sophisticated forecasting and modeling disciplines.

Capacity planners vary widely in their ability to understand and interrelate computer system resource needs with activities of the larger enterprise. The successful capacity planner must not only understand the tools, which are formidable, but also the data. Some capacity planners come from a systems programming and performance management background; others come from business and systems analysis.

Perhaps the most diverse array of technical analyses used in capacity planning involves various mathematical and logical techniques used to predict future system behavior. If you understand just this one thing about capacity planning, then you are ahead of the game: Capacity planners talk about what is *likely* to happen, not what *will* happen. They deal in things that cannot be measured or predicted with complete accuracy. The usual reason is that there are too many details to measure them all or that some of them haven't happened yet.

As business and government enterprises became dependent upon computer systems and computer networks to operate, the need for planning became more important. In the area of mainframe computing, where a single computer system can cost millions of dollars, it is imperative that this system be adequate to meet the demands of the enterprise—when the demands are greatest. The experience of management in the face of immensely complex computer systems has taught them a lesson on the value of being forewarned about developing capacity issues. Too many expensive surprises can be deadly.

Capacity forecasting stems from management's need to know what is likely to happen in the near and distant future. It should be an effort dedicated to providing managers with insight regarding the operational impact of current and anticipated MIS-related activities in future operations. The benefit of professional capacity planning is that it provides an effective aid for plotting future hardware, software, and information systems strategies. In addition, it is an explanatory activity. It attempts to answer the question of *why* we running out of capacity.

Computer systems and networks permeate every aspect of human activity involved with information. In today's information economy the computer system is often the most critical component of a business plan. The medium of value is information. Many businesses are profitable by simply repackaging available (for free) public information; others consolidate the details, or illuminate the structure, of data that would otherwise be uninteresting. As businesses become "on-line," the need for high availability, reliability, and time-sensitive operating environments develops. To run out of disk space, CPU, memory, or any other resource unexpectedly, especially when it is critical to the enterprise, is extremely costly. Today's computer systems, whether they be tiny PCs (alone or in a LAN) or mighty supercomputers (again, alone or in a system complex, sysplex, or system network), must not be "too much, too little, too soon, or too late" for the task.

There is no standard definition of capacity even within the context of capacity planning. Rather, the definitions of capacity depend on the behavior of interest and the system components being studied. For example, one definition of capacity may be stated in requests per unit of time, as in jobs per second, transactions per second, millions of instructions per second (MIPS), or bits per second (for network components). Another definition of capacity may be the maximum number of a certain workload unit (users) that the system can support while meeting a specified performance objective (a certain response time). One may talk of the *usable capacity* as compared to the *theoretical capacity* (nominal capacity). Perhaps the two most central ideas of capacity involve how quickly something can be done (throughput as the rate at which something can be done by the system or network) or how much can be done (the number of users or workload units—the system load). Given this wide spectrum of meanings for the capacity of a system, it is no surprise that many people may ask, What is capacity planning?

It is frequently unclear to management what kind of questions are best answered by capacity planning. Questions such as How many tape drives do we need for the next two years or Will our computer disk system support our business plan? are clearly capacity planning issues. Questions such as, How many initiators do we need for the MVS/ESA operating system so that users don't complain about their jobs waiting to run? or Do we have enough tape drives to avoid critical workload delays due to allocation recovery? appear to be systems programming or performance management questions (and may require expertise in these areas to answer them); however, they are capacity issues as well. It is often management's job to determine the impact and likelihood of running out of capacity in some resource and therefore to set priorities as to which resource is most critical and what planning or analysis activities should be done.

1.2 CAPACITY PLANNING—ART AND SCIENCE

Capacity planning is a whole-brain process and utilizes both the subjective and objective dimensions of consciousness—the feelings and the facts. Planning requires judgment, and judgmental activities necessarily require both the abilities to analyze components and synthesize components into a whole. The objective dimension of capacity planning may include complex mathematical analysis involving forecasting techniques, statistical analysis, or causal analysis (modeling). Typically, information is analyzed for the purpose of ferreting out patterns or trends. In addition, the quantification of many nonquantitative items of information may be required. For example, estimating the probabilities that some projects will be approved and that others will fail should be stated in the capacity plan as well as the related anticipation of growth or decline in various business activities that affect workloads, systems, and networks. The subjective dimension of capacity planning relies on intuition and experience to make expert guesses about near and distant future developments. Judgment, operative in this intuitive domain, departs the narrow confines of insufficient data and makes a leap toward wholeness and order. This is the art of planning.

Forecasting is an essential dimension of capacity planning. The forecasting process involves three modalities: *judgmental,* which is primarily intuitive and looks at historical milestones and patterns of human behavior in the organization as well as the marketplace in which the business functions; *causal* forecasting, in which elements that directly cause increase or decrease in computer resource consumption are analyzed, simulated, or modeled; and *analytic* forecasting, in which mathematical methods are utilized to

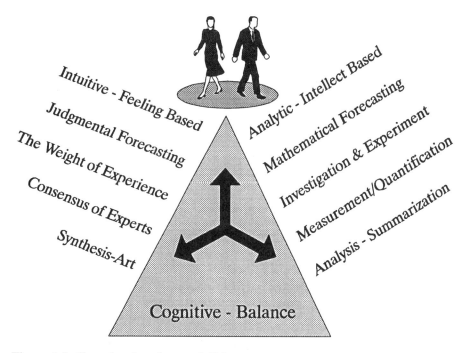

Figure 1.1 Capacity planning modalities

identify trends or causal patterns (see Figure 1.1). These distinctions, however, are not rigid. For example, judgment is required in both causal and analytic forecasting techniques. One must make judgments as to which statistical model or simulation is appropriate. Likewise, in forming a judgment, one must compare quantities and perform a logical analysis of events.

Generally, there are six basic elements of the capacity management process as proposed by Mullen [1].

- *Measurement Base*—The measurement base provides information on current configuration and resource usage. Numerous key indicators of utilization may be needed to define critical resource factors. Appropriate measurement tools, as well as definitions of the needed measurement elements, are required for the planning process. Capacity planning will not be successful without knowledge of the existing system behavior in terms of both service levels being delivered and utilization levels of the current resources. The measurement process is ongoing and continuous, with various levels of summarization to provide data reduction.

- *Database of Measurement Information*—Not only must measurements be available, but they must also be accessible and manageable. Data management is critical to avoid being overwhelmed with too many details. The database maintains historical information and allows the analyst to investigate past performance and analyze trends using statistical methods. Even simple data extraction and reporting functions will be greatly improved by access to an appropriate database. The database will contain utilization data for the various components of the computer system, as well as workload measures and the resources used for various workload categories.

- *Workload Characterization*—An accurate categorization of workloads enables the analyst to make capacity planning decisions regarding scheduling constraints, volume of work, resource profiles, and similar considerations on an application basis.

- *Service-level Deliverables*—These are formulated in terms of timeliness and accuracy. On-line systems, for example, may highlight the need for response time at a certain minimum level for business objectives to be achieved; batch processing frequently would focus on the delivery of printed output (reports, checks, publications, etc.) within a specified time period. The capacity analyst must be able to evaluate the actual service levels being delivered as compared to future projections and capacity constraints.

- *Analysis and Projection*—This requires the use of modeling or simulation tools and statistical analysis of the measurement data and business element processing volumes. Together, these may be used to forecast future growth and the impact on computer resources of new applications. Rather than requesting that business managers estimate internal DP measures, such as CPU time, I/Os, or the like, the analyst requests that they provide indicators that they use to report the activities of the business. Normally, a regression analysis is used to develop a model that relates the business elements to the application's resource utilization.

- *Management Reporting*—This is a critical element of the capacity management function and often the first priority. Management reporting provides information on current service-level deliverables, forecasting, and system configuration information. Service levels should be presented in terms of the volume of tasks processed and related capacity metrics, such as number of transactions processed (throughput) and response times achieved for those volumes. Potential exposures and alternatives are often presented as well.

The capacity planning process is both iterative and continuous in response to changing conditions in the business and the response of MIS in providing service.

1.3 THE PLANNING PROCESS

The planning process for complex computer systems environments involves both a scientific dimension and an artistic one. The science of planning includes all the complex analytical techniques available in computer science and statistics. The art of planning requires an understanding of human nature and the ability to distinguish ceremonial and organizational posturing from actual planning for action. The preparation for an increased probability of certain events over others—such as Heisenberg's Uncertainty Principle, which states that measurement may affect the measured—also shapes what is planned. The bottom line for the capacity planner and for the businessperson, is that the business is prepared for a *probable* future (or, if not, that we are aware of being unprepared). The capacity plan is a continuous process, although there may be a formal document prepared relative to budgeting or some other organizational event of interest. Typically, capacity planning must come into play in evaluating numerous scenarios of future possibilities.

The performance analyst and systems programmer are often masters of a blizzard of system details and take comfort in the precision of both their measurements and plans. The capacity analyst, however, must frequently develop large-scale plans, using uncertain and unmeasured information. In addition, this must be done quickly. It is not uncommon for the capacity planner to utilize extremely generalized rule-of-thumb techniques when pressed for rapid answers. As planning unfolds, the analyst may constantly revise salient assumptions to the scenario being examined. Flexibility and the willingness to guess are critical. Accuracy and precision, when warranted by the data, are also equally critical.

The capacity planning process consists of five primary activities as analyzed by Howard [2]:

1.   Identifying all workloads that the system must support
2.   Profiling each workload in terms of its resource demands and time interdependencies
3.   Aggregating the workloads
4.   Determining the aggregate resource requirements
5.   Finding equipment to match the aggregate resource requirements

Workload identification can be challenging, since a single program may also execute in multiple workloads due to differences in the amount of data processed. Examples of a simple workload categorization scheme could include:

Facility	Batch, Timesharing, On-line, Real-time Monitor
Environment	Scheduled/Priority, Distributed/Central
Status	Production, Development, Test, Systems Maintenance
User Function	Accounting, Manufacturing, Research, DP, Telemetry, Fire Control, Tracking, Training

Each workload must be quantified in terms of its resource consumption, its duration, and its placement on the time line according to Howard. The consumption rate is determined for each type of physical resource (bytes per hour × instructions per second, so many megabytes of memory, etc.). Duration of the workload may depend on device speeds, such as batch process-ing, or be relatively independent (as in scheduled on-line workloads).

The scale of the time line (24 hours is his recommendation) affects both the identification and the quantification of workloads. This is the basic operating cycle of the DP function. Howard recommends that the workload definition be done first, before defining the time line, to avoid overlooking a workload or incorrectly assessing its quantitative impact. The granularity of time durations, the number of workloads identified, and the resolution of the time line will determine how well the peaks and valleys of resource consumption show up on a resource-time graph.

Aggregating workloads can be done on the basis of resource demand over time for various resource categories such as the disk I/O channel resource. Once the aggregate demand can be determined, the interdependencies of event timings and resource consumption rates can be used to confirm the workload definitions or to indicate a need for redefinition based on the resolution of the sizing time frames or conditions. The aggregated work-loads thus give an indication of the quantities and capacities of equipment required to support the workloads for a given set of service-level objectives.

In selecting equipment to meet workload requirements, Howard men-tions several important factors. The most important factor is system architec-ture. This is the basis for assumptions regarding operating system overhead, tolerance limits for device performance, and the presence of specific con-figuration components. The applicability of multiprogramming using multi-ple CPU "engines," contingency capabilities, redundancy, upgradability, environmental requirements, and life-cycle expectancy are examples of the tradeoffs and considerations for selecting equipment.

1.4 EVALUATION OF FUTURE SCENARIOS— THE SPECTRUM OF PROBABILITIES

It is vital for the capacity planner to be able to quickly analyze probabilities and the consequences of various alternative scenarios of future computer configuration growth or decline. Traditionally, capacity planning has re-volved around two central domains of human cognitive activity: the *intuitive-subjective-synthesis* (ISS) orientation and the *acquired-objective-analysis* (AOA) orientation. The ISS activity focuses on the intuitive ability to understand the politics of experience within the organization and to discern which events are likely to transpire. Events of interest include organizational cheerleading, promises, agreements, and deals that are made within the company or between the company and other companies, customers, and employees. The intensities of human feelings are seen as the motivational energy of the organization. In contrast, the AOA orientation is focused on analyzing trends or patterns from the past with the expectation that these historical patterns will develop in the future as well. There is a desire to use the morphology (form) of events, made analytically tractable by measurement and emotional detachment, in order to control or forecast events that are isomorphic (similar in form). The first orientation favors a social dimension of capacity planning. It is certainly true that one cannot plan in isolation, only looking at data from the past. One must survey the users of the information systems environment, the business conditions and volumes, and the entire economic continuum that surrounds the enterprise. From this, one may identify the external and internal factors that could affect the dynamics of computer workload variation. For example, user surveys solicit forecasts of future requirements for disk space, tape storage, CPU time, etc., and any other cost-related items. Forecasts are often requested in the natural forecasting units of the business itself, such as number of accounts, number of paychecks, sales volumes, etc.

In collecting forecast information from users who are not computer experts, one typically finds that the variance and error in their forecasts, relative to actual, is much too extreme. Short-term requirements tend to be very exact, since people can quantify a project that is ongoing or about to be put "into production." Long-term requirements are usually quite vague, and people generally don't know where to begin to estimate what their requirements will be. Often, the capacity planning function must help demonstrate, usually in graphical form, the previous patterns of use in order to establish norms for future scenarios. The capacity planner provides statistical estimations (for example, the average CPU time required to process one "customer"), which are used to estimate future customer volumes.

As we move from simple to complex (indeterminate) considerations, the quantitatively validated components in our models decline in favor of judgmental factors—we begin to replace fact with opinion (a *defactualized* model). The greater the reliance on deductive, as opposed to empirical or inductive, components, the greater will be the expected error in our models. The emphasis here is *expected* error. We are forewarned, and forewarned is forearmed. The technical analyst, often uncomfortable with mere opinion (except, of course, "expert" opinion), is forearmed by giving explicit credit to the unpredictability and inherent complexity of the situation. It is not uncommon for the MIS executive to listen to a long litany of disclaimers, critical assumptions, and numerous limitations before getting any advice regarding computer resource needs.

The primary analytical instruments associated with capacity planning are:

- Statistical inference processes
- Simple simulation techniques
- Bayesian estimation processes
- Regression, correlation, time-series, or harmonic analysis techniques

A general characteristic of these instruments, in terms of their informational results, is that they generate a range of possible solutions or probabilistic estimates, which are assigned some index of confidence. Computer systems, including the relationship between computer systems and the larger enterprise in which they function, are *moderately stochastic*, that is, the basic causal relationships are known, but databases are often incomplete or not available—hence, the parametric uncertainty.

Since the capacity planning analyst is concerned with forecasting or the prediction of factors pertinent to MIS operations, the underlying assumptions of these techniques (and the problems in using them) are:

- The assumption that future values will be the product of their historical behaviors
- Nonlinearity
- Codeterminacy of state variables
- Nonrandomness of error terms

The assumption that future values will be generated from past behaviors is not always warranted. For example, in planning for a new application workload a more appropriate technique would be modeling the new workload in order to predict the effect it will have on system performance and capacity. Alternatively, for businesses that have slow growth in overall volume and a representative historical base of measurements is available, then time-series analysis or linear regression may be quite effective.

Simple linear regression based on the passage of time as the predictor variable will often lack predictive utility with nonlinear distributions. This will become more apparent as more data become available for analysis. Measures of "fit" will usually indicate problems in applying linear trend functions to nonlinear data.

Codeterminacy of state variables can be due to multicollinearity (for the independent variables) or autocorrelation (for the dependent variable), which means that the variables are not statistically independent from one another. For example, it is not surprising that the hourly average *maximum* number of tape mounts would be related to the average hourly number of tape mounts or that the number of rental cars owned by a car rental agency would be highly correlated to the square footage of available parking spaces leased by the agency.

Nonrandomness of error terms, in a statistical forecast, frequently indicates a pattern to the data called heteroscedasticity. The variance of the error in the model must be constant. If successive values of the *same* error term are variable, then we are not justified in using common linear models.

Which analytical instrument is applied by the analyst is determined by the properties of the problem under study and by determining which technique promises to yield the desired (or maximum) amount of information with the lowest expenditure of analytical resources and/or time. This ability usually comes from the experience of having used these techniques successfully in the past. In recent years, expert systems, which help to select the correct model for data analysis, have been developed. These expert systems achieve this by either (1) analyzing data distribution characteristics (such as a test for normality), or (2) running multiple models in a "tournament" to see which have the least error or best fit, or (3) some combination of both techniques.

1.5 CAPACITY PLANNING AND PREDICTING THE FUTURE

The capacity planner is not a fortune teller and his or her ability to forecast is really the ability to synthesize the assumptions, anticipations, and forecasts of others, as well as the analytical dimension of extracting future probabilities from known patterns of historical usage. Hardware plans, software plans, systems configurations, and cost projections are the ultimate result of forecasts. Typically, business planning involves multiple scenarios. In one scenario, the economy improves, the business improves, business volume goes up, and more capacity is required. In others, there is a flat trend and very little growth and, in still others, general decline.

Experienced businesspeople can usually provide reliable estimates of short-term business volume requirements. Where possible, one should be able to convert business volumes into computer resource requirements through a process of natural unit forecasting techniques. Projecting growth, even with the most sophisticated methods, is difficult. This is primarily due to the fact that each organization's growth experience is strongly influenced by outside forces. In addition, users tend to underestimate growth (or vastly overestimate). Perhaps the most frequently overlooked growth factor is *stimulation*—the growth caused by user acceptance of a new capability that significantly exceeds expectations.

The role within the corporation or enterprise of capacity planning is quite variable. In many small MIS environments, capacity planning is considered only an occasional event, which one performs when approaching a critical level of resource usage for some very expensive component (such as a mainframe CPU). In very large environments, capacity planning is included with other technical services functions.

It is very unusual to find professional capacity planning being done in the decentralized MIS organization. In many decentralized organizations, the MIS function is at best a corporate function, which provides guidelines and technology assessments from a highly strategic level. Decentralized systems, such as mid-range computers and PC/LANs, are managed by different groups that usually avoid cooperative global planning. They have little incentive and few rewards to do so.

The factors that affect capacity planning will also affect the ability of capacity planners to provide usable, clear, and accurate predictions and associated resource plans. There are numerous specific considerations that influence the capacity planning activity, as outlined by Cook [3]. These factors can be categorized as technical, organizational, or managerial.

1.5.1 Technical Factors

- *Hardware and Software Components*—The capacity analyst must have a clear understanding of how hardware configurations are connected, as well as their capabilities for multiprocessing, file sharing, device switching, teleprocessing, etc. He or she should be knowledgeable about the operating system and related software in order to make appropriate decisions about software changes.

- *Workloads*—Workloads are categorized such that they are documented, batch and interactive workload are not mixed due to their different resource profiles, they are easily understood, and the system performance required is made explicit.

- *Workload Trends*—Trends and patterns of change are analyzed from historical data. This data should be collected on an applications basis. The analyst will use this data to identify workload peaks, seasonality, and sudden increases in resource usage (step functions) caused by adding business volume, new applications, or new groups of end users.

- *Modeling*—Many proprietary models are available for simulating how the system and its components would respond to changes in workload, software, or configuration. It is a much less expensive alternative to actual benchmarking on existing or new equipment.

- *Capacity Measures*—Consistent use of standard metrics, such as CPU utilization, MIPS ratings, ITR ratings, site normalized resource units, service units, etc., enables capacity planning to be done in a way that is understandable to MIS management.

1.5.2 Business Factors

- *Physical Planning Constraints*—Here, various physical environmental limitations and considerations come into play. New systems or changes to existing systems must be within the context of physical accessibility (cable length limitations, for example), flooring and weight considerations, air conditioning, electrical power, plumbing (for water-cooled mainframes), and similar environmental factors.

- *Contingency Plans*—Resource symmetry or fault tolerance by avoiding single point of failure configurations may be required to ensure recoverability from an outage. Recovery may be within the site (partition or domain recovery on MVS systems) as well as off site. These concerns may result in more equipment than would otherwise be necessary based on capacity considerations alone.

- *Scheduling Constraints and Critical Workloads*—The capacity planner must be aware of critical windows for throughput-sensitive batch or response-sensitive on-line systems. The scheduling constraints of these workloads frequently require excess capacity during noncritical time periods in order to meet peak service-level requirements.

- *Tuning Efforts*—Some MIS environments have achieved as much as a 300 percent improvement in throughput for batch processing by diligent I/O tuning. Application- and system-level tuning can create (or reclaim) significant processing capacity. These kinds of substantial changes in system performance must be considered as a cost-effective alternative to system upgrades or additions.

1.5.3 Management Factors

- *Business Units and Plans*—Business units or business elements (also called the natural forecasting units or key volume indicators) are business volumes that should relate to the workload classifications. These business indicators may be such events as orders processed, widgets sold, tax forms prepared, etc., and are the units for planning used by the business managers. Statistical methods are employed by the capacity planner to forecast computer resources based on the relationship between one or more business units and critical resources, such as CPU utilization, CPU usage (hours), data storage, etc.

- *Service Levels*—Service levels are measures of the quality of service provided, such as timeliness (response time, turnaround time, etc.), accuracy (errors, reruns, etc.), reliability, and cost. As the capacity of the system is constrained, service levels may become unacceptable. Where possible, service-level agreements may provide more explicit definitions of service-level requirements and cost-recovery mechanisms.

- *Latent Demand*—Latent demand is the demand on the system that is not being made due to restrictions of existing system capacity or the limitations of the application software. New resources may unleash this pent-up demand and consume the excess capacity in such a way that resource exhaustion takes place much faster than expected. To avoid this, the capacity planner must be able to estimate this latent demand.

- *Management Policies*—Management policy may focus and limit the choices available, such as manufacturer, levels of reserve capacity, compatibility with existing systems, or disaster recovery plans. These should be documented in the written plans and recommendations of the capacity planner.

- *Life Expectancy of a Configuration*—MIS managers frequently prefer two or more years between significant purchases or upgrades due to the disruption of service and impact on business capital associated with such changes. Thus, the capacity planner must provide recommendations that explicitly address the life expectancy of the new or additional resource, taking into consideration both current and forecasted needs.

- *Formal Resource Plans*—The formal documents prepared by the capacity planner should include management recommendations, key assumptions, the methodology used, the cost of doing nothing, and the cost and timetable of implementing the plan. This plan should be reviewed and changes evaluated on a periodic basis.

- *Changing Plans*—The capacity planner must be able to quickly change elements of the formal resource plans in order to accommodate new information, such as the introduction of new workloads, different service-level requirements, hardware changes, etc.

1.6 CAPACITY PLANNING AND PERFORMANCE MANAGEMENT

One machine can do the work of fifty ordinary men.
No machine can do the work of one extraordinary man.

— Elbert Hubbard

It is not uncommon for both management and the technical staff to define capacity planning as just another complex task to be included within performance management. This is probably because both performance management and capacity planning require an understanding of global system dynamics and use similar tools and data.

In capacity *planning*, the focus is on the future (planning), while capacity *management* emphasizes the problem of ensuring that the presently available computing resources are used efficiently. For capacity planning, the likely outcome is the recommendation of different computing resources, while for capacity management the alternatives are those of adjusting usage patterns, rearranging the configuration, or changing system parameters (performance tuning) in order to maximize system performance. Although performance management is very complex and the subject of numerous scholarly papers, it is only a small part of the capacity planning problem. A central issue of capacity planning is that of cost, which includes the total cost of implementing the computer system or systems, network or networks, as deemed necessary by the enterprise.

In performance management there is also a forecasting dimension—for example, in modeling the probable performance of given changes planned for a system's configuration or its components (causal reconstruction). However, the skills necessary for performance management and as well as its objectives are quite different from capacity planning. Like capacity planning, performance management is an ongoing process. System tuning efforts are reiterated over and over again because systems never stay in tune for long. Likewise, since capacity constantly changes, capacity planning is reiterated over and over again. The data analysis performed by the performance analyst is very short term and geared toward specific behaviors that are expected from the system, whereas data analysis for the capacity planner tends to be much longer term and assumes the performance constraints are constant.

The statistical forecasting techniques used by the capacity planner assume that the workloads being measured over time are essentially invariant and have the same logical identity; however, most application workloads are under continuous maintenance and "enhancements." Some statistical techniques that accommodate this would be from the area of weighted linear regression or exponential smoothing where, for example, one can use a mathematical process to favor recent data over older, "more distant" data. The relationship between the volume of natural units (e.g., the number of paychecks, accounts, or widgets) and the patterns of system resource consumption (e.g., CPU time, disk space, tape mounts, etc.) changes noticeably with the application functions. Ideally, the application workloads provide an electronic or algorithmic analog to the corresponding business activity (the correspondence of informational/algorithmic processes to business enterprise dynamics). Alternately, one may describe the relationship between the application program and the enterprise as having a structural isomorphism or at least correlated behaviors. Despite these hoped-for ideal relations between information system structures and the activities of the enterprise, it is not at all unusual for the primary resource-intensive activities of application systems to be focused on technology factors alone—for example, managing the interface between incompatible file structures, data formats or other system properties. In these cases, the relationship between business units and resource consumption units may be complex, nonlinear, and/or negligible (and, in the long term, a good candidate for "reengineering").

If the performance analyst can be viewed as focused on the components and dynamics of short-term system behavior, then the capacity planner can be viewed as focused on the longer-term system ecology. A system ecology includes those properties that give the system a determinable form sufficient to separate it from its environment (the boundaries, organizational or otherwise, of MIS). This encompassing "without" of system boundaries—typified in the use of business volume values for predicting system behavior rather than merely past states of MIS workloads (as defined by MIS)—is important to the capacity planning analyst in order to determine that nature of the system's interchanges with the larger enterprise. How well the MIS organization "weathers" these interchanges not only tells us a great deal about future capacity considerations but also the viability of the MIS organization itself to be "placid" or "turbulent" within its ecology.

The behavior of computer systems, although deterministic at a component level, is less deterministic at an ecological level. Workloads arise, grow, and decline in response to factors often beyond the control of MIS. If the MIS organization is strategically important to the larger enterprise, then its welfare is codeterminate; thus the capacity planner, in this context, is motivated to characterize forecasting activities as *actionable*, i.e., a basis for action and not merely a budgeting scenario. The ability of MIS management to direct subsequent action depends on the number of alternatives outlined and their degree of difference in qualitative terms. The usual condition of scarce resources makes it impossible for MIS to preadapt to many, signifi-

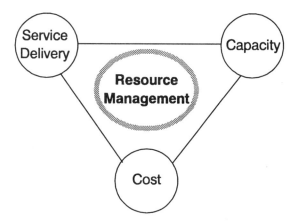

Figure 1.2 The mission of resource management

cantly different, alternative events assigned significant probabilities of occurrence. An upgrade plan for a mainframe environment, involving millions of dollars, does not present hundreds of alternatives for executive management. Only those alternatives are presented that fall within a range or confidence interval allowed by probabilistic informational models. Thus, the capacity planner constructs models to serve several ambitions: explanation, description, prediction, causal reconstruction, and prescription.

Capacity planning may be considered as part of the mission of resource management. Cost, service and capacity are interrelated by mutual constraints. Service objectives require a certain level of capacity to be achieved, yet at an affordable cost.

1.7 CAPACITY PLANNING AND BUSINESS PLANNING

I hope to obtain grant money, of course.
After all, it is better to have a permanent income than to be fascinating.

— Oscar Wilde

Because of the cost orientation of capacity planning and its use of business elements in forecasting, the capacity planning function is very closely interdependent with business planning and business forecasting. The underlying hypothesis of a business element forecasting methodology is that the volume of business activity may be related to the demand for computer resources. Using a statistical model, estimates of the volume of future business activity may be directly translated into specific quantities of computer resources. For this reason, the capacity planner evaluates models that use one or more business elements as an independent variable. The essential motivation for this approach to forecasting is that both the business community and the capacity planning analyst recognize the importance of using a systematic approach to computer workload forecasting as a function of business activity (see Figure 1.3).

Once a forecast is possible that relies on business activity (X amount of computer resources required for y amount of business activity), then cost projections, in the form of natural units, are possible. For example, in allocating the costs of information systems back to the organizational components that use it (chargeback accounting), the invoice could be in terms of reports, accounts, widgets, or some other unit that is an element of the business activity, rather than in terms of computer metrics (CPU time, disk

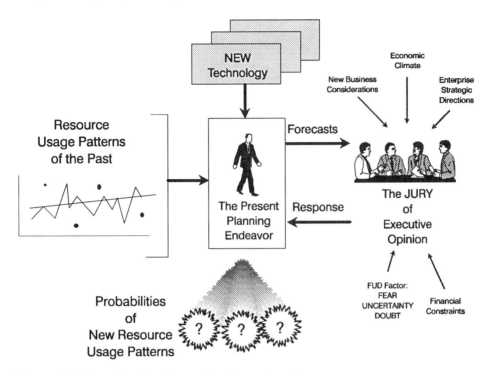

Figure 1.3 Capacity planning and business planning

space, tape mounts, etc.). Unfortunately, the relationship between natural units and computer resources may be variable, requiring periodic adjustments in the chargeback rates. This is due to several factors:

1. The business application software is undergoing constant maintenance and other changes (as mentioned earlier).

2. The computer configuration itself is undergoing changes (additional equipment is installed, upgraded, or replaced).

3. Accounting is also sensitive to the passage of time (e.g., depreciation schedules, lease agreements starting/ending, etc.)

Effective capacity planning is interrelated to budget planning. The business analyst may say, How much will it cost to support scenario *X* or scenario *Y*? or You tell me how much it will cost to implement plan *Z*. The capacity planner, on the other hand, may want to respond to budget plans: You tell me what you want to do; I'll tell you what it will cost. Unfortunately, that

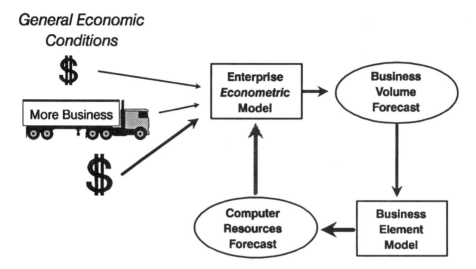

Figure 1.4 Model relationships

information (what it will cost) may have the effect of revising the budget. Of course, there is the unbudgeted and unplanned "business opportunity." If I can make $20 and it will cost me $5, then do it now and worry about the budget later (after you collect the $20). This is fine as long as there are no "surprises," such as a $50 cost for computer-related support, previously unknown to the businessperson. When it begins to cost $50 to collect $5 you quickly go out of business (end game/log off).

In some very large enterprises, especially those with substantial research and develop resources, it is possible to examine the business from an econometric perspective. General econometric models may be used to predict future business volume (see Figure 1.4). These forecasts can then be used as input to computer resource forecasting models. The cost profiles for future computer systems requirements may, in turn, be input to the original economic assumptions of the enterprise econometric model (this will in turn impact capital costs projections).

1.8 REFERENCES

1. Mullen, J. William, "Capacity Planning: Basic Elements for the Process." *CMG Conference Proceedings,* 1985, pp. 468–474.

2. Howard, Phillip C. *IS Capacity Management Handbook Series.* vol. 1. Phoenix, AZ: The Institute for Computer Capacity Management, 1992.

3. Cook, J. "Capacity Planning Checklist." *Computer Performance,* 5 (December 1964): pp. 222–228.

2

The Metrics of Capacity Planning—Foundations

You never know what is enough unless you know what is more than enough.

— William Blake,
The Marriage of Heaven and Hell [1790–1793].
Proverbs of Hell, line 46

2.1 FUNDAMENTALS

The primary metrics of interest in capacity planning are *utilization metrics,* i.e., a measure of the percent of time a resource is busy or in use for a given load level. Utilization may be expressed as the ratio of busy time to total elapsed time. Thus, if a computer is busy for 30 minutes and idle for 30 minutes during a 60-minute (one-hour) observation period, we would say the computer is 50 percent utilized or has a utilization of 50 percent for that hour. Generally, other measures are employed using the mean or average utilization in order to determine a generally characteristic summary of the usage of the resource. For example, the average utilization per hour for on-line systems to represent to management a "typical" day or the *average maximum utilization* per hour and *average minimum utilization* per hour may be graphically combined to show the dispersion or variability of the mean values (see Figure 2.1). Successive averaging of sampled measurements will tend to reduce the amount of data to be reported and flatten the overall

23

CPU Hourly Utilization

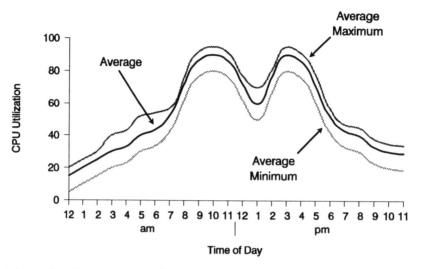

Figure 2.1 A comparison of average maxima minima variation

appearance (reduce variance). Average utilization over critical service periods may be summarized on monthly or even quarterly levels in order to show trends or growth patterns over longer duration than typically used by performance analysts.

The utilization of any device, without resorting to the more complex mathematics of queuing theory, can be expressed by the utilization law. A general mathematical expression of the utilization law is:

$$U_i = \frac{B_i}{T} = \left(\frac{C_i}{T}\right)\left(\frac{B_i}{C_i}\right) = X_i S_i \tag{1}$$

where

C_i is the number of completions
B_i is the busy time of device i during observation period T

$$\text{Throughput } X_i = \frac{\text{Number of Completions}}{\text{Time}} = \frac{C_i}{T}$$

$$\text{Mean Service Time } S_i = \frac{\text{Total Time Served}}{\text{Number Served}} = \frac{B_i}{C_i}$$

This expression of utilization has the advantage that no assumptions need be made about variable distribution or interarrival times.

Other metrics, more often used in performance management, are supportive of various definitions of capacity, including:

- *Response Metrics*—The time between arrival of a request for service and its delivery. These are data that deal with duration, such as response time or turnaround time.

- *Productivity Metrics*—Throughput as the number of requests per unit of time. These are data that deal with the number of items such as queue length, number of MVS initiators, or number of VMS processes. Also included in this category are data that deal with rate (occurrences of something per unit of time).

2.2 RESOURCE CATEGORIZATION

Computer system resources may be categorized as *physical* or *abstract* (see Figure 2.2). Examples of physical resources would be the central processing unit, real storage (as compared to "virtual" storage), and the I/O compo-

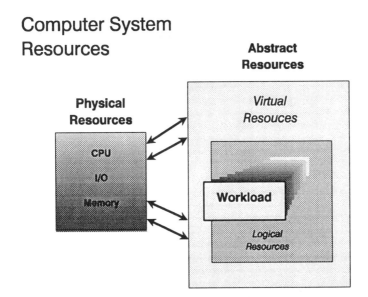

Figure 2.2 Physical and logical resources

nents such as tape and disk drives, controllers, and related equipment. The physical resources are also referred to as "platforms" on which processing is manifest (workloads).

Abstract computer resources include *virtual* and *logical* resources. A virtual resource usually refers to the range of addressable storage encompassing the architecturally defined maximum of the computer system. In MVS systems this would be an *address space*; in DEC/VAX systems, an *image*. The operating system enables the address space description and the activation of programs within the virtual storage. The objects referenced by application programs are, in effect, translations or mappings from real objects to their virtual counterparts. The virtual objects and their composite structures define the *logical* resources of the system. In virtual storage systems, even data—the fundamental unit of data management being a file or data set—correspond to virtual objects, such as *data set control blocks* (MVS).

The abstract resource environment of mainframe systems has evolved a multitude of analytical techniques for workload-oriented measurement. One example is *execution-state analysis* where each address space is examined at regular intervals in order to derive a distribution of *execution states* (active, idle, delayed, contention, etc.). Use of this technique can help the analyst understand emerging constraint conditions and assist in refining capacity projections. As physical resource becomes inadequate for a growing abstract workload, upgrade paths are evaluated by the analyst.

Measurement takes place at many levels within the operating system and creates measurement data. This is true for almost all operating systems. The vendor may provide these with the operating system software or as a separate billable item. The capacity planner, like the systems programmer and performance analyst, needs information that describes the basic measurements to determine how much of each system resource was used for each work unit, an overview of how the system is performing, and the relationship between system capacity and workload activity.

Like the systems programmer, the capacity analyst views the activity of the system from the perspective of *workloads*. A workload may be described as a list of service requests to the system or, from a modeling point of view, as the probability of various requests. For simulation modeling, a workload may be described as a trace of requests measured on a real system. For business element forecasting and cost analysis, a workload may be described as activity of the system associated with a specific application (or in support of that application), including such abstract entities as subsystems, multiuser single address spaces, batch, interactive processes, or some combination of these that defines the application system boundaries.

Workload characterization is the process of identifying all those elements of system activity that share some profile of interest. The average behavior of each workload component is characterized for modeling purposes by *workload parameters*, such as transaction types, paging activity, I/O service requests, etc. It is the parameters that depend on the workload and not the system that are the salient components of the model. For example, a workload may be characterized by the CPU time used for a given CPU model (or normalized across some range of CPUs with known speeds) or by the average block size for I/O activity. Elapsed time (how long it ran) is not an appropriate parameter, since it depends on the system on which the workload is executed (an idle system versus a busy system, for example).

Workload characterization at a detailed analysis level requires using several analytical techniques used in statistics. These techniques are covered later in Chapter 5 of this book.

According to Mohr and Penansky [1] there are two basic approaches to workload characterization, *resource-oriented* and *activity unit-based*. The resource-oriented approach is focused primarily on the hardware utilized and ignores the application or type of processing being done. The activity unit-based approach concentrates on the application or type of processing being done and translates these to resource utilization forecasts. Artis [2] points out that both approaches to workload characterization depend on the partitioning of the workload into a set of classes that display some degree of homogeneity. The resource-based approach is most applicable to the forecasting of existing workloads and the activity unit-based approaches are more appropriate for new applications. Artis recommends the following measures for identifying workload characteristics:

- *Counts*—Used in all activity unit-based approaches, you count the number of jobs or steps, the number of on-line transactions or tasks, the number of terminals, etc. Each unit is characterized by its individual resource consumption.

- *Resource Consumption*—This is simply the measurement of all system resource components such as the CPU, memory, channels, etc., for each workload.

- *Computer Resource Unit*—This is a composite measure of resource consumption that combines the usage of individual resources into a single value. Artis does not recommend this measurement for determining specific resource problems, but it may be appropriate for job accounting systems.

- *Works*—This is a software physics measurement unit, defined as a unit of data that is moved by a processor from one storage device to another. This is most advantageous in that it is a unit of measurement that is invariant with respect to the system on which the workload runs.

- *Exterior Resource Consumption*—This is a measure of resources external to the central processing unit and memory such as tape drives, disk mounts, forms changes, etc. Artis does not find this general enough to characterize the entire workload; however, it is used to quantify the demands on these peripheral resources.

Additional attributes that Artis recommends for use in the partitioning process include mode of operation, resource usage, schedule, organizational function, location, and service class. More than one attribute may be used and there is no *best* way to characterize a workload.

In order to analyze the workloads in a rigorous and analytical manner for purposes of partitioning, Artis recommends cluster analysis. Cluster analysis is a statistical technique used to identify clusters in an n-dimensional space. For the purpose of workload clustering, the n-dimensional space is the resource space (or set of all resources under consideration) where n is the number of resources. For example, taking the two-dimensional case of real storage and CPU seconds, a set of jobs might appear as shown in Figure 2.3.

Cluster analysis is a useful technique for forecasting and benchmark generation as well as for identifying outlying values. The specific resource category used would depend on the objective of the study. Examples of resources might be CPU seconds, tape mounts, print lines, memory required, I/Os by device type, etc. Cluster analysis techniques are covered in Chapter 5 of this book.

Activity unit-based workload characterization is based on type of work. The units differ from one type of work to another due to the differences in characteristics of the various types of work performed. Artis recommends some general categories for this type of characterization:

- *Batch*—The batch environment has both a variable part related to input volume and a fixed portion that is forecast on the number of runs. The variable part is the application unit. If the batch workload has no easily defined application unit, then the average batch job is used as the forecast unit.

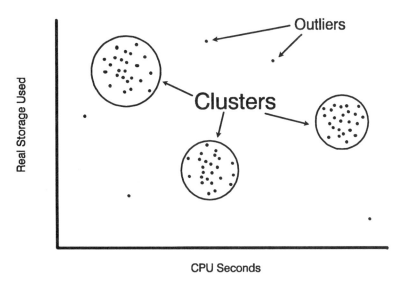

Figure 2.3　Cluster analysis

- *Time Sharing*—Artis recommends the "session," defined as the period of time from log on to log off, as the unit for characterizing and forecasting this workload. Due to the variation in session length, it is recommended that several sessions be defined based on length or application. This will help separate the different types of sessions. Alternatively, different types of timesharing may be defined by the type of activity, such as engineering, financial analysis, technical writing, etc.

- *On-line Applications*—For individual application workloads of this category the unit of characterization is the number of transactions of various types. This is similar in concept to batch workloads. An average resource usage per transaction is recommended unless different types of transactions differ significantly in their resource use. For the latter case, separate forecast units for each type may be defined.

- *Block Time*—This is an unusual unit for capacity planning except as applied to the capacity to schedule a workload. The forecast unit for block time is the elapsed time that the system is to be used by the workload. A historical base of measurements is the source for forecasting workloads in this category.

- *Non-machine Work Functions*—This is a strictly operational category, which identifies work functions that do not involve the computer system itself. The usual forecast unit is the number of "events" or activities of a particular type. Examples of this category would be data entry output handling. In order to be useful for computer system workload forecasting, the analyst must discern the relationship between computer-related forecast units and nonmachine work functions. Each work function must be analyzed with considerable care.

Because of the close relationship between computer system capacity planning and performance management, it is useful to look at how workloads are categorized for performance evaluation. Jain [3] maintains that the most crucial part of any performance evaluation project is the workload. Naturally, his focus for characterizing workloads is resource-oriented. Although his procedures include averaging and clustering as techniques for workload characterization, he also discusses additional techniques, such as dispersion, principal-component analysis, and Markov models.

Measures of dispersion include the standard deviation, the variance, the coefficient of variation, etc. Other alternatives for describing the variability are range, percentiles, quartiles, and the mean absolute deviation. The importance of using these measures is to identify groups of activity for which variability is very high. High variance across resource parameters indicates that the grouping is not effective. If, for example, the coefficient of variation is very high, subdivision into several classes would be warranted.

Principal-component analysis is used to classify workload components by the weighted sum of their parameter values (resource consumption values). Using a_j as weight for the jth parameter x_j, the weighted sum of y is

$$y = \sum_{j=1}^{n} a_j x_j \tag{2}$$

This sum can then be used to classify the components into a number of classes, such as low demand, medium demand, or high demand for the resource of interest.

Principal-component analysis allows finding the weights w_j's such that y_j's (the principal factors) provide the maximum discrimination among the components. This analysis produces a set of factors $\{y_1, y_2, \ldots y_n\}$ such that:

1.   The y's are linear combinations of x's:

$$y_i = \sum_{j=1}^{n} a_{ij} x_j \tag{3}$$

2. The y's form an orthogonal set; that is, their inner product is zero:

$$y_i, y_j = \sum_k a_{ik}a_{kj} = 0 \tag{4}$$

3. The y's form an ordered set such that y_1 explains the highest percentage of the variance in resource demands, y_2 explains a lower percentage, y_3 explains a still lower percentage, and so forth.

For further details of this technique, the interested reader should consult a book on factor analysis, for example, Harmon [4].

2.3 RESOURCE CONSUMPTION METRICS

As mentioned earlier, the primary metrics of interest to capacity planning are the utilization metrics of response time and throughput. Let us explore these concepts more closely, paying special attention to the various types of subcategories for each.

Response time is the interval between a request for service from a system or system component and the response. This can be applied to processes involving users of systems or the components of systems themselves:

Process Type	Response Time Definition
On-line Systems	The interval between user's request and the system response
Device Subsystems	The interval between system request for I/O and disk response
	The interval between system request for tape mount and the response of a robotic tape subsystem.
Client/Server	The interval between client request for I/O and server response

Response time metrics are most often used in establishing *service targets* for the system, such as an on-line response time of no greater than two seconds for X-type CICS transactions during a certain time-of-day period $T_{x \text{ to } y}$. Response time is sensitive to system load and increases as system load increases. *Service level administration,* from the perspective of performance management, is focused on the achievement of the target response time of the system by controlling system load (e g , number of batch processes or jobs running, system resource management adjustments (in MVS), or other means). The maximum achievable system load under the constraint of such a service target response time is called the *nominal capacity* of the system.

Insofar as response time represents a process consisting of all those events between the start of a request and system response, it is of interest to the capacity planning analyst to be aware of the need for response time decomposition not only relative to the capacity of the system to achieve a target response time under a given load level but also in terms of the capacity of subsystem components. Let us therefore examine the composition of typical system and subsystem response time components.

A request for service is a process that requires time to enact (it is not instantaneous). For an on-line system, the start of the request may involve filling in a screen or panel, selecting options for a complex query, etc., and finally pressing a button to enter or transmit the request. Likewise, the response of the system or system component (in the case of device response) is a complex, multievent process. The time between the end of the user request and the beginning of system execution is the *reaction time* of the system. The system may need to perform a variety of internal tasks, such as virtual storage management (paging, swapping, queuing) before it can execute a response. The beginning of the system response may require allocation of network or communication subsystems, which, in turn, may add additional activities to the overall response time (network management, for example). During the execution of the response, I/O activities are usually required and thus the system may, in turn, become the user of numerous I/O subsystems. Finally, the system response is completed and transmitted (see Figure 2.4).

Within today's computer systems environments, the I/O storage hierarchy is the source of most response time concerns, since data retrieval is a large component of database and on-line query systems typical of business activity (see Figure 2.5). For example, if the actual 10-nanosecond response time of a 3090 mainframe high-speed buffer is considered on a more perceivable scale of one second, then the much slower disk response time—assuming a not-too-busy 3380 disk is responding at 25 milliseconds—is 25 days! More and more mainframe systems applications designers are attempting to explore the use of memory, especially expanded (or extended) storage for data access (data in memory). This technique was also explored in earlier days using arrays (FORTRAN) or working storage (COBOL) in an attempt to avoid I/O to slower devices. I/O avoidance is the most promising technique at this time for improving the performance of I/O-intensive applications.

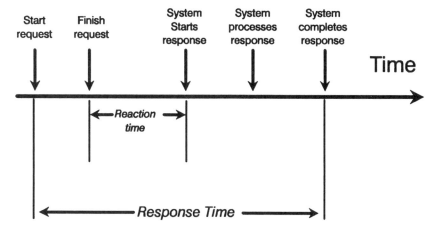

Figure 2.4 Response times

For the batch (noninteractive) environment, *turnaround time* is the interval between the submission of a batch job (IBM) or process (DEC) and its completion (this includes the time to read and process data). Where on-line systems have a reaction time measured as the interval between when the user finishes his or her request and the system starts execution of the request, the batch environment would define reaction time as the interval between the time a job or process is submitted and the beginning of its execution (see Figure 2.6).

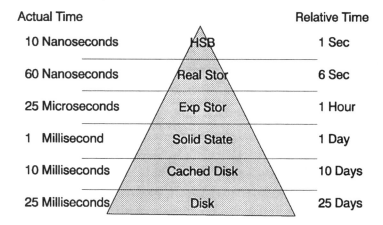

Figure 2.5 Storage response hierarchy

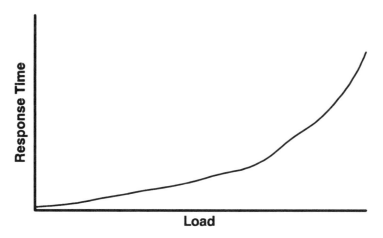

Figure 2.6 System capacity and response time

Throughput is the rate at which the requests of the system can be serviced. Examples of throughput would include the following:

Workload Type	Metric
Batch	Jobs per second
On-line System	Transactions or requests per second
Networks	Packets or bits per second

The capacity planner may also be interested in the corresponding business volume metrics for throughput, such as:

Business Elements	Metric
Reports	Rcports printed per day
Customer Requests	Requests processed per hour
Database Searches	Searches per day
Revenue Generated	Revenue per minute (for cost outage analysis)

Throughput increases as load increases up to a critical threshold. This threshold is the *nominal capacity* of the system (see Figure 2.7). Then, it begins to decline as more and more activity of the system is concentrated on managing the arrival of new work (workload management), queue management, and job/process tracking.

In reporting utilization, response, or productivity metrics, management wants to know the typical value. Most analysts (and almost all managers)

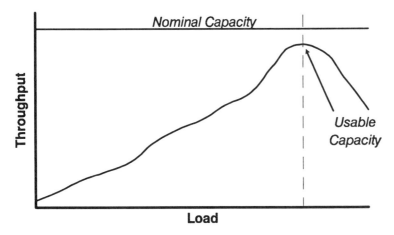

Figure 2.7 System capacity and throughput

equate "typical" with "average" and thus proceed to determine the mean value. The issue of representativeness, for reporting purposes, can fill volumes on statistical theory. When looking for the "typical" in a distribution, in the sense that it is representative of the whole, it is good to be aware of how the mean or average value can be very misleading.

For many metrics, mean value is overemphasized. However, do not overlook the importance of the effects of variability, and do not confuse "typical value" with mean or "average" value. For example, most on-line systems, for a given time zone, exhibit the Double Hump Curve, as shown in Figure 2.8.

In this theoretical example, the mean value is actually the low point and is not a typical value. It is not what most people who use the system are experiencing. Since, in many instances, the mean value—as a measure of central tendency—is requested by management as a way of determining what a typical value is, it is important that the capacity planner report not only isolated statistics but a feeling for the whole distribution of values. In this example, the more typical value is the two maximums or modalities of the distribution.

Capacity planning is usually applied to mainframes but is increasingly applied to mid-range systems as well. It is uncommon to use capacity planning for PCs or other low-cost components of an information system. Capacity planning is itself somewhat costly. It requires the services of experts, complex data analysis, and other nontrivial undertakings. Nevertheless, critical PCs serving as file servers in a business-critical context can be the subject of professional capacity planning.

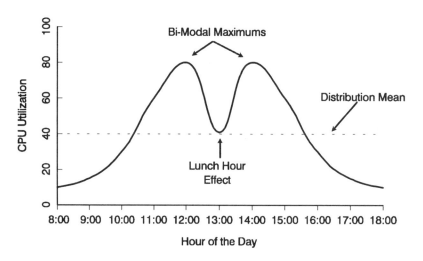

Figure 2.8 Double hump curve

The trend in the early 1990s seems to be toward mainframe-like capabilities on small and much less expensive computer systems. It is tempting for the businessperson to believe that these smaller systems can be managed cheaply as well. However, without appropriate systems management disciplines and the unmanaged growth of departmental systems, businesses of the next 20 years may be faced with catastrophic complexity, uncertain capacity, and uncontrollable costs.

Any computer system component that, through lack of resource capacity, can negatively impact on business activity should be included in capacity planning activities. This is also true of networks (although it is not as common as mainframes).

2.4 RESOURCE USAGE AND PERFORMANCE LEVEL METRICS FOR CAPACITY PROJECTIONS

Resource usage and performance level metrics are not normally associated with capacity planning as such; however, they can be used to assist the capacity planner by identifying situations where operating anomalies could be perpetuated into the future. Capacity requirements projection should be based on workload growth forecasts applied to a reasonably tuned system. This is especially true when evaluating analytic models of the system to determine short-term effects of changes in workload or configuration. Independent forecasts for the main hardware resources such as processor, main storage, disk (I/O rate, path and actuator traffic intensity, and actuator space) should be put into the context of the resource relationship metrics that represent usage level dependence.

According to Criner [6], competitive benchmarking looks to best practice, regardless of the nature of the work being done. This is in contrast to workload benchmarking, which is used to determine which hardware configuration best meets a fixed data processing load. Competitive benchmarking studies are provided by several vendors which compare the performance of datacenters to determine the best practice and to establish and validate process goals for process improvement. Very large companies, such as IBM, which utilize several datacenters, will often use internal benchmarks, i.e. comparing datacenters to one another within the same company. Benchmarking provides a basis for performance evaluation and helps develop a strategy for improvement. The primary value of benchmarking is perspective. It lets the data processing installation know how it is performing relative to industry norms.

As an example of commonly applied resource usage metrics, the following list has evolved from several studies to represent installation specifics that enhance the reasonability of capacity planning projections. These are especially well summarized and updated by Major [5]. When a datacenter's usage parameter falls considerably outside the norms, they should ask themselves why that is so.

2.4.1   Relative I/O Content (R) of Workloads

R is the workload's propensity to generate disk I/O operations as the relevant code is being processed. The disk I/O rate (S) and the CPU busy (B), when measured for a recurring workload of a system image over sustained periods of time (usually a period of one to three weeks during which no major change in workload composition or supporting software occurs), are in a more or less constant ratio relative to a measure of processor throughput capacity (M):

$$R = \frac{S}{M \cdot B} \tag{5}$$

This number has been changing over time and had an average value of 1.0 in 1980 and became 0.25 in 1991. It continues to decline as large systems continue to exploit I/O avoidance techniques associated with relational database systems, data-in-memory, and large cache capacities.

Some reasons for a high R-value, relative to industry standards, are:

- main storage shortage, possibly confirmed by high paging/swapping rates
- fully normalized relational tables or nonindexed attributes in relational tables
- software limitations that do not permit exploitation of main storage
- improper use of system parameters that forces I/O when main storage is available
- usage patterns that limit the use of system facilities designed to avoid I/O

Some reasons for a low R-value, relative to industry standards, are:

- Compute-intensive workloads such as scientific/engineering applications that primarily using main storage resident data (e.g., arrays)
- Multiple system images use a significant part of the available processor resource such that the measured image is not heavily favored

Some earlier works which explore the relative I/O content metric can be found in [1], [2], and [3].

2.4.2 Access Density (AD) of Disk Resident Data

AD, as defined in [4], is the propensity of disk resident data to result in disk I/Os as the workload is being processed. The access density is defined in terms of the ratio of disk I/O rate (S) over the shared disk configuration and that configuration's nominal gigabyte capacity (DG) as follows:

$$AD = \frac{S}{DG} \qquad (6)$$

Major [5] reports some reasons for high/low *AD* values of interest to the capacity planner.

Some of the reasons for high *AD*-value are:

- main storage shortage, possibly verified by higher than normal page/swap I/O rates relative to the total DASD I/O rate
- higher than usual data packing levels on DASD
- high level of DASD caching

Some of the reasons for low *AD*-value are:

- good exploitation of Data-In-Memory software options with generous size main storage configured.
- political assignment of DASD volumes to "owners" with concomitant separation of departmental data at the expense of empty DASD space

2.4.3 Process Density of DASD Resident Data (PDD)

PDD represents the processing cost (per second) that is associated with having on-line 1 gigabyte of nominal DASD capacity. It is defined in terms of the quanta/second processing rate (*Q*) over the shared DASD configurations nominal gigabyte capacity as follows:

$$PDD = \frac{Q}{DG} \tag{7}$$

where

$$Q = M \cdot B \tag{8}$$

As DASD resident data continues to move under the control of storage management software, PDD is expected to increase. In addition, PDD will be high for installations with higher data manipulation requirements.

2.4.4 Process Density of Memory Resident Data (PDM)

PDM represents the processing cost (per second) that is associated with having on-line 1 megabyte of nominal Main Storage capacity. As an installation's processing requirements grow over time, its process density of memory decreases. *PDM* is defined as the installation's quanta/second processing rate (Q) over the total configured megabytes of Main Storage (MS):

$$PDM = \frac{Q}{MS} \tag{9}$$

2.4.5 Data Remoteness Factor (DRF)

DRF represents the ratio of on-line DASD resident data gigabytes to the Main Storage resident gigabytes. It is defined relative to the proportion of the total DASD nominal gigabytes (DG) to the total configured gigabytes of Main Storage (MS) times a loading factor (0.50 for the 1990–91 estimate). Converting to a common scale (Main Storage is usually defined in megabytes) gives:

$$DRF = 500 \cdot \frac{DG}{MS} \tag{10}$$

2.4.6 Memory Access Density (MAD)

MAD represents the ratio of DASD I/Os (S) to the nominal Main Storage megabytes and is defined as follows:

$$MAD = \frac{S}{MS} \tag{11}$$

or

$$MAD = R \cdot PDM \tag{12}$$

As I/O avoidance techniques, such as Data-In-Memory, are utilized more and more, this number will decrease. Major [5] reports an adjusted average value for North American installations as 1.38.

2.5 RESOURCE EXHAUSTION

Computer system resources have a finite capacity. Detecting resource exhaustion, or, better yet, forecasting it, is an essential activity of capacity management. Inevitably there comes a time when upgrades or replacements appear to be the only option. It is essential that the capacity analyst be able to substantiate the full economic benefit of such action and that less costly alternatives be explored. It is not surprising that management will most often want a solution that not only meets current needs but also the expectations of the near future.

Forestalling these options frequently becomes a major concern before getting executive management approvals for the megabucks required. Whereas the performance analyst may routinely focus on workload tuning, during times of resource exhaustion the focus switches to tuning the system.

As we have seen from earlier discussions, the capacity of a system is defined in terms of service. The scheduling of that service is often constrained by business requirements (the customer-driven environment). Workloads that cannot be rescheduled, response times that cannot be improved with system tuning, and unacceptable batch throughput conspire together to motivate MIS to look at increasing the capacity of the bottleneck resource. It is at this point that vendors are consulted regarding upgrade options, additions, trade-ins, replacements, and costs. Unfortunately, it can be a difficult situation in which to bargain for a good price if the seller knows that you are desperate.

What are some options to adding capacity via purchases? If workloads are movable (there is often excess capacity in the wee hours, for example) or a portion of the workload can stand delay, this is a possible option to buy some time. More high-priority work can be added to the system until resource queuing compromises acceptable service.

Backup systems may be utilized, if available. If multiple data centers exist within the company, workloads may be relocated geographically, assuming the necessary data communications are in place (less costly than the alternatives). Definitions of "acceptable" service may be changed and service-level agreements renegotiated (or terminated).

Often, simple alternatives to adding more capacity are not acceptable, and the intricacies of configuration changes become prominent. One likely and unpleasant surprise of adding another CPU is the software costs associated with CPU-based (rather than "site") licenses. Floor space considerations may intrude, and along with floor space are the costly environmental changes that may be required for very large systems. For example, heating, cooling, and power requirements may double.

Quick and cheap solutions may be traps. Technology has a way of leading one into dead ends. A vendor may provide very low-cost suggestions to buy processor model X only because of their intentions to drop support for it in the near future. Or, processor model X may be incompatible with the latest whiz-bang disk subsystem. The technology strategy of the business must be considered in the upgrade process. A capacity solution today may become a boat anchor to progress tomorrow. It is not unusual to find that the low-cost opportunity for adding capacity is unacceptable due to configuration constraints in which the benefit is short lived. Sometimes, the strategies of mainframe vendors may tie new peripheral capabilities to a new technology mainframe, forcing customers to upgrade if they want to make use of the features or capacity of the new equipment.

Many factors affect equipment acquisition decisions: technology changes, business operating conditions, workload growth and workload management, and financing opportunities. Of these, the financial considerations are the most significant in terms of impact to the operating environment. Capacity analysts need to understand return on investment goals and other financial concepts in order to assist in negotiating the specific terms of hardware acquisition.

2.6   REFERENCES

1. Major, J.B., "Capacity Planning and the I/O—CPU Equation," *Proceedings, G.U.I.D.E 26,* June, 1985.

2. Major, J.B., "Capacity Planning with a SIO Methdology," *Proceedings, SHARE 65,* August, 1985.

3. Ryden, J.C., "Trends in Processor, I/O and Storage Usage," *Proceedings, UKCMG '89,* May, 1989.

4. Bannister, A. G., "Configuring IBM 3990/3390 Using Access Density," *CMG Conference Proceedings, CMG '90,* December, 1990.

5. Major, J.B., "Resource Usage Metrics and Trends: Host Systems," *CMG Conference Proceedings, CMG '92,* December, 1992.

6. Criner, James C., "Benchmarking Data Processing Installations," *Capacity Management Review,* 22:3, March, 1994.

3

Business Elements and Service Levels

3.1 METHODOLOGY

The underlying hypothesis of a business element forecasting methodology is that the volume of business activity in the enterprise served by the information systems organization may be related to the demand for computer resources [1]. Furthermore, the methodology assumes not only that this relationship exists but also that it may be quantifiable. Using a statistical model, estimates of the volume of future business activity may be directly translated into specific quantities of computer resources. This technique allows business managers to forecast their requirements in terms that are familiar to them rather than in the metrics of computer usage or utilization. It is usually desirable by senior management to be able to transform these business plans into their corresponding computer system requirements without significant risk of being off target with respect to costly computer resources. The most common procedure for this process is linear regression analysis.

The linear correlation coefficient should be calculated and a scatter diagram created to indicate the strength and nature of the relationship. The sample correlation coefficient r is computed by the formula:

$$r = \frac{\sum xy - n\overline{x}\overline{y}}{\sqrt{\left(\sum x^2 - n\overline{x}^2\right)\left(\sum y^2 - n\overline{y}^2\right)}} \tag{1}$$

where

n is the number of items,

$\overline{x}$ is the mean of x, $\overline{x} = \dfrac{\displaystyle\sum_{i=1}^{i=n} x_i}{n}$

and

$\overline{y}$ is the mean of y, $\overline{y} = \dfrac{\displaystyle\sum_{i=1}^{i=n} y_i}{n}$

$$\sum xy = \sum_{i=1}^{n} x_i y_i \quad \text{and} \quad \sum x^2 = \sum_{i=1}^{n} x_i^2$$

When two variables x and y are correlated, this simply means that they are associated in some way, so that if one changes, the other also changes. The correlation coefficient, r, reflects the strength of this association.

A simple linear regression analysis may predict the computer resource required. In addition, it will provide some indication of the predictive accuracy, using cross-validation of the historical data, of the predictor variable. The sample regression line is of the form

$$y = a + bx \tag{2}$$

where

$$b = \frac{\displaystyle\sum_{i=1}^{n} x_i y_i - n\overline{x}\overline{y}}{\displaystyle\sum_{i=1}^{n} x_i^2 - n\overline{x}^2} \tag{3}$$

and

$$a = \bar{y} - b\bar{x} \tag{4}$$

In equation (2), y is the predicted response (e.g., CPU hours, megabytes of disk storage, etc.), and the predictor variable is x (e.g., the number of widgets, accounts, or other business element).

The best linear model is given by the regression parameters a and b, derived from the data, which minimizes the sum of squared errors:

$$\sum_{i=1}^{n} e_i^2 = \sum_{i=1}^{n} (y_i - a - bx)^2 \tag{5}$$

subject to

$$\sum_{i=1}^{n} e_i = \sum_{i=1}^{n} (y_i - a - bx_i) = 0 \tag{6}$$

A variety of models, other than linear, may be investigated. Additional models that are often useful include the exponential, mutiplicative, reciprocal, and multivariate models.

Linear Model: $\quad\quad\quad\quad y = a + bx$

Exponential Model : $\quad\quad y = e^{(a+bx)}$

Multiplicative Model: $\quad y = ax^b$

Reciprocal Model: $\quad\quad\quad \dfrac{1}{y} = a + bx$

Multivariate Model: $\quad\quad y = bx_1 + cx_2 + \ldots + nx_n$

If Y_{est} represents the value of Y for given values of X, as estimated from the least-square regression line of Y on X, a measure of the scatter about the regression line is supplied by the standard error of estimate:

$$S_{y,x} = \sqrt{\dfrac{\sum_{i=1}^{n} (y - Y_{est})^2}{n}} \tag{7}$$

The standard error of prediction at the 95 percent level is $1.96S_{y.x}$ and is the main factor in computing a confidence interval. The closer the upper and lower confidence interval values are to the forecast line, the better the fit.

For planning purposes, it is recommended that this kind of analysis be combined with other statistical studies and the results of simulation models of expected workloads.

3.1.1 Identifying Business Elements

The first part of a natural forecasting unit approach requires developing a business element model that identifies the business elements. These usually must be obtained from users. This is the most difficult part of the methodology and requires interviewing developers of the applications to determine the characteristics they believe have the most significant influence on the resource requirements. From this process we can form a conceptual overview of the logic of the system. The next step involves an iterative process of interviewing users of the system to determine how they measure their system usage levels. In order to successfully implement the statistical methodology, it is necessary not only to identify possible business elements, but to obtain historical observations of these elements for correlation to the historical patterns of use.

3.1.2 Statistical Analysis and Modeling

The next phase of a business element analysis applies statistical procedures to relate, or correlate, historical observations of business data with computer resource use. This analysis leads to developing a model representing computer resources as a function of the values of the business elements.

Use of a common time scale is required and is critical to the use of the statistical correlation process between historical resources statistics and historical business element data. Using multiple linear regression, estimates for the following business element forecasting model can be determined:

$$y = a_0 + a_1 X_1 + \ldots + a_n X_n \tag{8}$$

Where Y is a historical resource consumption element (e.g., CPU hours); $X_1, X_2, \ldots, X_n$ are values of user reported business elements; $a_0, a_1, \ldots, a_n$ are coefficients that relate business elements to the resource element; and a_0 is an error term containing the residual difference between the linear combination of the coefficients and the observed values of the business elements.

3.1.3 Validating the Business Element Statistical Model

Model validation has basically two dimensions: (1) the mathematical appropriateness of the statistical model and (2) the actual ability of the model to provide realistic forecasts. In the first case, we must examine the mathematical properties of the variables, their distribution, and their relationship. In the second, we must examine the results relative to actual measurements.

To judge the mathematical validity of the statistical model, four basic assumptions must be determined:

- $X_1, X_2, \ldots, X_n$ *must be statistically independent.* This implies that each business element represents a unique data point that cannot be expressed as a function of one or more of the other business elements. The failure to satisfy this assumption implies that the model cannot determine which of several related business elements have predictive power on the dependent (computer resource) element.

- *The theoretical mean value of the error term is zero.* This implies that there are no other factors influencing resource consumption besides sampling and data error.

- *The error term has a constant variance.* A variance is a statistical parameter that controls the amount of dispersion of a variable about its mean value. A constant variance indicates that the size of the error term is bounded in probability; that is, the probability of seeing an error greater than a specified value is small.

- *The error terms are statistically independent of each other and of the independent variables* $X_1, X_2, \ldots, X_n.$ This assumption assures us that the model contains all the factors that influence the dependent (computer resource) variable. The assumption is violated when there is a systematic pattern to the error terms in the model. This problem is known as autocorrelation.

Deciding which business elements to include in the model can be done with stepwise regression techniques to ensure a model based only on the business elements that have the strongest predictive power. Typically, the analyst cannot wait for some future time—a year or more—to determine predictive accuracy. Rather, given a sufficient historical data base, the first half can be used to predict the second half and vice versa. This is called cross-validation and is a common technique used by statistical forecasters. This will help establish the predictive validity of the model using the data given. The objectives of cross-validation are:

- Determine the predictive power of the dependent variable (computer resource)

- Enable prediction of changes in computer resource(s) as a result of changes in business elements

- Provide good estimates of future values of the dependent variable (based on statistical probability)

3.2 SERVICE LEVELS AND OBJECTIVES

Service levels are categories of measurable system behavior that are highly correlated to the service objectives of the MIS organization. Each system provides a set of services. Knowledge of the services and outcomes is important in selecting the right metrics and workloads for *service-level administration*. In general, the metrics of service levels are quantitatively related to *speed, accuracy,* and *availability* of services. However, the larger enterprise will also insist on *qualitative* measures as well, such as providing services that are *useful, strategic, innovative, competitive,* and *flexible.* The MIS organization will typically eschew any service-level categories that are outside its control.

The objective of MIS is to serve the larger enterprise. In this sense, MIS is a system contained within a larger system and interrelated to other critical service providers (e.g., postal system, telephone system, etc.). As a service provider, MIS will attempt to operate in such a manner as to achieve the target values, within some range, of its service levels. These *service-level targets* or goals are the measures of good service. In essence, they represent the bounds within which service is recognized to be acceptable, identify what services require attention (e.g., tuning, renegotiation of agreements, upgrades, additional resources, etc.), and indicate when enough attention has been accomplished. Senior management would prefer, most likely, to have a service goal of providing the best possible service at all times within the constraints of current resources and budgets. Unfortunately, this is too vague for the MIS organization. MIS must quantify "best possible," for example.

3.2.1 Examples of Service Goals

- The average transaction response time for X subsystem will not exceed two seconds during prime shift hours with less than 70,000 transactions

- Ninety-seven percent of all production batch jobs for customer Y will complete by 8:00 A.M. each day, Monday through Friday

- During prime shift, 98 percent of all service-level goals will be accomplished

- CICS will be available no less than 98 percent of prime shift

Service-level goals can be classified, as defined by their scope of application, into three basic categories: guidelines or heuristics, service-level objectives, and service-level contracts.

Guidelines or *heuristics* are statements of service-level targets that are used for control actions within MIS in order to support more public or formal statements of service. They assist MIS in determining how well service is being provided to its customers. The heuristic nature of these guidelines is due to the fact that goals are susceptible to alteration—a process of *successive improvement,* where MIS may learn from both successes and failures (for example, system tuning). The criteria for success and failure may vary with what MIS has previously learned or what it expects to be able to learn in the future.

Service-level objectives are service goals that are formal, documented, and recognized in some official way throughout MIS. The customers may, or may not, be aware of these objectives. They are used to approach the problem of organizational control from the standpoint of system coordination, integration, and operation. The modality of this control paradigm is that of the cybernetic control model(see Figure 3.1). This approach has great merit when applied to essentially moderately stochastic problems within any organization.

Here are the operational attributes associated with the cybernetic control model of service objective monitoring and control:

- The service levels are the processes that we are interested in controlling.

- Preselected, critical parameters of the process are to be monitored constantly by a set of appropriate monitors. These may be real-time

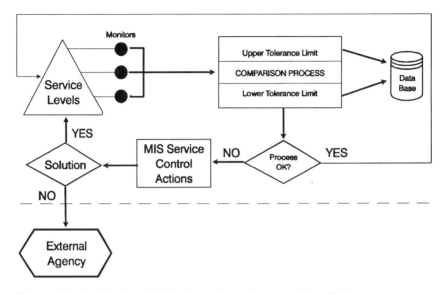

Figure 3.1 Service-level objective cybernetic control model

system monitors, as well as statistical data. The sensors capture the point-in-time values of the critical control parameters of service.

- These values are then evaluated by some kind of comparison process to determine if they are within some preestablished, tolerable limits.

- Next, there is a decision that must be made: Are the values associated with the MIS processing activities within or outside the permissible limits of good service? If they are within limits, then nothing further is to be done—wc sct our control system ready to receive the next readings from the monitors. If the actual values are not within permissible limits, i.e., both the magnitude and direction, then we must take some action to provide a service solution.

- We next compare the actual departure from the tolerance limits against a range for which we have error-correction procedures available (e.g., adding page data sets, reconfiguration of disk resources, etc.). Insofar as MIS has anticipated an occasional deviation from the service objectives, a process is initiated to bring the service back within tolerable limits.

- If MIS does not have a solution, the closed system of this somewhat automated process must be broken, and a call for help is initiated to a superordinate (e.g., a decision-maker equipped to handle the situation—usually a level above the MIS management). This person must then take some sort of judgmental action:

1. Take the problem to the next higher level

2. Make a correction in the process, altering basic objectives for future runs

3. Alter the sensors

4. Alter the permissible tolerance limits

The capacity planner is called upon to evaluate what the system is capable of providing in terms of *service-level capacity*. The capacity of the system must be adequate but not excessive. As with most human endeavors, clear goals are necessary to accomplish this.

3.3 SERVICE-LEVEL AGREEMENTS

Service-level agreements (or contracts) represent an explicit statement of the level of service that will be delivered to the customer at a given unit cost. It is also usually a bilateral contract in which the customer agrees not to request any more than some specified level of service (number of jobs, transactions per unit of time, volume, and/or time constraints against some baseline). Different customers of the same service provider may negotiate for different levels of service, with cost accounting or chargeback making adjustments in cost according to those levels. Failure to meet service goals by MIS may result in reduced costs to the customer and failure of the customer to stay below a given baseline may result in higher charges. For internal customers (MIS is in-scope of the enterprise or "in-sourced"), these costs are, more or less, artificial cost-recovery mechanisms that motivate management to be accountable for controlling costs and service. For external customers (MIS is out-of-scope of the enterprise or "out-sourced"), these costs are real and have an impact on the balance sheet of the customer.

A service-level agreement is a formal document and may be structured according to the demands of senior management within the enterprise. Typically, the agreement will have five major sections. These include a prologue, service details, the standard offerings of MIS, the performance objectives, and how award points are determined.

The first section, or *prologue*, will include a statement of intent of the agreement. It states that MIS will provide certain services as detailed later in the document, and, in exchange, the customer will agree to cooperate in forecasting future resources to deliver these services. There is also usually some statement that the letter of the document will not undermine the spirit or intent of facilitating the business or activity of the enterprise. Next, a change procedure is included, which describes how the agreement may be changed, how change is initiated, reasons that are acceptable for making changes, etc. This section of the document also includes a statement of responsibilities, such as who will be responsible for reviewing performance measurement statistics, how the customer will provide growth information for planning and cost adjustments, and how often this will be done.

The next section describes the *service details* of the agreement. The application system is described, including what benefits it provides to the company. The customer community is described, including its locations within the organization as well as geographical locations. Representatives are identified for all the parties of the agreement, including the customer, the contractor (MIS), the primary customer, primary contractor, customer representative, contractor representative, and any facilitors of the agreement. Next, a schedule of service hours is listed, including services, if any, for weekends and holidays. Typically, production scheduling is critical to the applications within the scope of the agreement. Also, within this section, is included a definition of *natural units*. This is often the most difficult part of the agreement to determine. The agreement may be initiated with only a "best guess" of what these units are. In the case of natural unit billing for chargeback, these units are critical to both the cost accounting and forecasting areas of MIS. Identification of these units requires statistical analyses that correlate business metrics to workload levels. Service charges determine the price of the service used for customer billing (associated with natural units), and, without predetermined natural units, which are cost sensitive, the price may be the cost (for internal customers) or the cost plus some profit margin (for external customers or if MIS is a "profit center").

The next section is the *standard offerings*. These identify the services of MIS that are included as part of all service-level agreements. They include customer support activities, such as records management (production control and migration, scheduled maintenance, emergency maintenance, restart and recovery, disaster recovery); security; and other considerations (system problems, i.e., hardware, system software, and communication/network outages).

The *performance objectives* section gives detailed information regarding the primary performance objectives of the agreements, their definitions, and methods of measurements. An example of a performance objective might be dependability (percent of uptime). Online systems are especially sensitive to availability. This may be referenced to a schedule for weekdays versus weekends, and, according to certain prime service hours for batch processing, a different measure of effectiveness may be employed, such as the timeliness of report delivery. In all cases the method of measure should be clearly stated.

The final section is the specification of *award points*. These points determine the evaluation of MIS in meeting the performance objectives. A range of points is specified for meeting the objectives according to "Best" (MIS exceeded the objectives), "Objective" (MIS met the objective or target of performance), or "Nonacceptable" (MIS failed to meet the minimum acceptable measures).

3.4 AWARD POINTS

The diversity of services offered by MIS is usually combined into one total or score of points (say, 100 points) with subsets of service (which add up to this total) weighted by the customer's priorities. These services include all the delivery-of-service parameters within the scope of MIS. The use of award points is a common nomenclature to describe these services. The target may be 90 award points (MIS is doing a "good" job) and a discount to the customer at 85 award points (MIS is not doing a "good" job and thus literally "pays" the consequences). Exceeding target (say, 95 points) is desirable. As an example, 30 points may be made for performance targets (response times, throughput, etc.), 40 points for availability targets of critical services, and the remaining 30 points divided among other services (reports delivered on time, checks mailed, orders processed, etc.).

Under this cost-recovery arrangement, customers who "recover" more costs will have a higher priority than other customers. Within a customer category, priorities are (theoretically) established by the award points. The service goals, as well as the costs, need to reflect as much as practical the customer's perception of service. In order to assure the less expensive customer receives "good" service, and to avoid playing favorites with high-profile customers, separate service goals for qualitatively different types of work may be established.

Because of the dynamic nature of ongoing services to a constantly changing set of business priorities, the service-level agreement will need frequent
review and revision.

What is the role of the capacity analyst in the establishment and administration of service-level agreements? Initially, the analyst must determine the
service goals that *can* be set.

Let us consider the case of response time service. For example, should the
response time for a certain class of on-line transactions be less than 1.0
seconds or less than 0.5 seconds? One approach is to correlate the response
time with the number of complaints about service, searching for that point
where there are essentially no complaints. The next question is can the
"no-complaint" level be met most of the time? A statistical analysis of the
distribution of service time by hour over a month or more could provide a
percentile distribution of response times. It would be realistic to promise
what at least 90 percent of the distribution exhibits, especially if this is a
value less than the point where the customers complain in significant numbers. Thus, the analyst derives a prescriptive initial value, which could be
recommended to management.

Batch processing is more complicated. Data must be analyzed separately
for the major resource classes of batch work. A scatter plot for a month or
more of data using CPU time and I/O volume could be constructed to
identify clusters suitable for use in establishing job classes (in this case a
two-dimensional resource space). If we included tape mounts and print
lines, we would have a four-dimensional resource space and thus leave be-
hind the capabilities of scatter plots and enter upon the more difficult
territory of statistical cluster analysis.

An example of an award point specification, in an agreement between
MIS and a financial systems department, follows. This agreement is typical of
large, complex environments. In this case, the environment includes multiple data centers and multiple networks.

Executive Summary

The Service-level Agreement between the Financial Systems Department and MIS contains the major objectives listed below. The objectives are weighted according to importance by assigning a Performance Point value to each. The total Performance Points available is 100. Each objective and the points earned are measured monthly with results reported to MIS management and Financial Systems management.

A. DEPENDABILITY

  1. **Percent of Uptime**

     Objective: The on-line system will be available as shown below:

Application	Mon.–Fri. Objective	Sat. Objective	Points	AWARD POINTS (Total)
Accounts Payable	98%	95%	8.0	
General Ledger Other	90%	90%	2.0	
Gen Ledger Monthly	98%	98%	6.0	
Gen Ledger Special	98%	98%	4.0	
TAX System	95%	95%	2.0	
Labor System	95%	95%	2.0	
Function Code	95%	95%	1.0	

Monday through Friday performance will receive 90% of the points, and Saturday will receive 10%.

Total Award Points—Percent of Uptime 25.0

B. ON-LINE TIMELINESS

  Objective:

	Points	AWARD POINTS (Total)
Access to system via 3174 controllers.		
≤ 3 seconds for 95% of Accounts Payable Transactions	6	
≤ 5 seconds for 99% of Accounts Payable Transactions	4	

				Points	*AWARD POINTS (Total)*
Access to system via X.25 packet switching.					
≤ 6.25 seconds for 95% of Accounts Payable Transactions				3	
≤ 11.0 seconds for 99% of Accounts Payable Transactions				2	

Total Award Points—Percent of Uptime   15.0

C.   BATCH TIMELINESS

Objective: For the reports listed in Appendix B the following delivery objectives have been set for each data center:

			Points	*AWARD POINTS (Total)*
Priority 1	Below Obj.	≤ 12:00 A.M.	1.0	
	Below Obj.	≤ 10:00 A.M.	2.0	
	Objective	≤ 8:30 A.M.	3.6	
	Best Perf.	≤ 7:30 A.M.		4.0
Priority 2	Below Obj.	≤ 12:00 A.M.	1.0	
	Objective	≤ 10:00 A.M.	1.8	
	Best Perf.	≤ 9:00 A.M.		2.0
Priority 3	Below Obj.	≤ 3:00 P.M.	0.5	
	Objective	≤ 1:00 P.M.	0.9	
	Best Perf.	≤ 12:00 A.M.		1
Priority 4	Below Obj.	> 2:00 P.M.	0.0	
	Objective	≤ 2:00 P.M.	1.0	
	Best Perf.	≤ 2:00 P.M.	<u>1.0</u>	

Total Award Points per Datacenter   8.0

Total Award Points—Report Delivery: 3 (data centers) × 8.0 =   24.0

D. FINANCIAL CLOSE TIMELINESS

1. **Trial Balances**

Objective: First, Second, and Third Financial Trial Balances, Final Regional Financials, and Final Sector Financials must be completed by the dates in the Closing Schedule. On these dates, the reports 4001, 7200, and 7210 are tracked within each region to determine if delivery objectives are obtained.

Objective: For the reports listed in Appendix B the following delivery objectives have been set for each data center:

			Points	*AWARD POINTS (Total)*
Below Obj.	delivered	12:00 A.M.	0.5	
Below Obj.	delivered	10:00 A.M.	1.0	
Objective	delivered	8:30 A.M.	1.8	
Best Perf.	delivered	7:30 A.M.	2.0	

Total Award available for 1 trial balance day in 1 data center is 2.0 points. With 5 trial balance days and 3 datacenters, the total award points for this Performance Item is:

2.0 (Award Points) × 5 (Trial Balance Days) × 3 (data centers) =
Total Award Points—Trial Balance   30.0

2. **Corporate Interface Tape**

Objective: The Corporate Interface Tape must be delivered by 12:00 noon on the date shown in the Closing Schedule.
    A delivery receipt is received from the Corporate Financial Department.

Objective: For the reports listed in Appendix B the following delivery objectives have been set for each data center:

	AWARD POINTS (Total)
Total Award Points—Corporate Interace Tape	6.0

TOTAL AWARD POINTS ALL PERFORMANCE ITEMS   <u>100.0</u>

3.5   COST CONTROLS AND CHARGEBACK

The capacity planner is frequently called upon to contribute in the areas of cost controls and chargeback or *resource accounting*. Since the capacity planner is focused on system resource capacity and utilization, these areas are also vital to determining the metrics for resource accounting. These metrics are, in turn, of primary concern to executive management in their attempts to assess and control the costs of MIS. The cost dimensions of interest to the executive are price per function, return on investment, and control (budgeting). The user perceives the role of capacity planning from a service perspective (response time and throughput), and the technician perceives capacity planning from a hardware/software/workload forecasting perspective. These differing views of capacity planning are all valid and are concurrent aspects of the function of capacity planning (see Figure 3.2).

The capacity planner must have some understanding of the primary business of the firm and how computing supports this business. In order to deal effectively with issues of resource accounting, there must be a focus on both the costs and the potential or realized returns. The acquisitions of MIS must

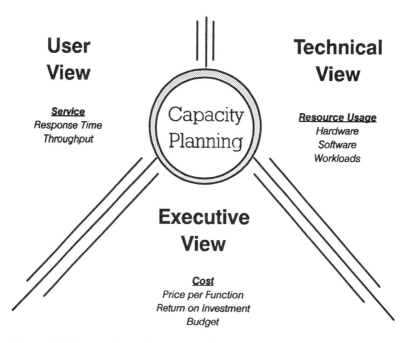

Figure 3.2 Three views of capacity planning

be viewed as investments. These investments are made to fulfill the goals of the business by providing necessary services. For example, the consequences of not meeting service-level objectives may be lost sales, lost revenue (due to inability to react), employee dissatisfaction, inhibited business growth, or violation of service-level agreements. Sometimes, even legal problems can arise due to nonperformance of the firm in its contracts. It is not unusual for the capacity planner to include cost and benefit information in proposals for new hardware, a given technical solution, or some combination of both, such as the reconfiguration of existing systems in order to accommodate new service requirements. The conversion or alteration of software licensing agreements (in order to implement various hardware changes) can radically affect costs. For example, either CPU or site licensing can provide potential savings depending on the specific configuration plans being addressed. The capacity planner, in order to assess the cost consequences of various configuration alternatives, must go beyond mere technical considerations of MIPS or memory and investigate numerous areas. Rosenberg [2] provides a helpful summary of many cost-related factors to consider in configuration analysis, including:

People Costs

- Expenditure of time and effort to implement to new configuration
- Implementation and reeducation
- Increases or decreases in headcount

Facility Costs

- Floor space changes
- Power requirements
- Cooling (air conditioning, chilled water, etc.)
- Site preparation

Supplies

Converting inventory items—e.g., decision to acquire new tape technology, may necessitate:

- New tapes
- JCL changes
- Data transfers

Overhead

- The indirect costs of personnel (vacation, education, space, insurance)
- Increase insurance for plant and equipment
- Additional phone lines
- Delivery of output

Cost determination is only one of the two principal components of resource accounting. The other is billing, i.e., bills sent to users, which may be based on something other than computer resources. Naturally, billing and cost are very interdependent. The users of MIS services will react most strongly (favorably or unfavorably) to the billing component of chargeback. The costing component of chargeback has five principal objectives, as outlined by Gewurtz [3]:

1. The cost categories must be *simple and understandable* by DP staff and users

2. They must be described in *DP terminology*

3. Costs should *control and account* for all hardware and software facilities and resources that the data center is responsible for in an equitable fashion

4. The costing methodology should be *consistent* year to year

5. Costing should *be an integral part* of the overall management information system and include the load forecast methodology, definitions of service-level objectives, capacity planning methodology, performance evaluation methodology, business plan, and budget process

In contrast to this, Gewurtz outlines the objectives of the billing component of chargeback. Billing is based on resource units or unit costs. These units may be related to a specific computer system resource, such as disk space; a business transaction (also called transaction unit billing, function billing, or natural unit billing) or on-line session; or may be based on a fixed price annual contract. The desirable objectives for the billing component, according to Gewurtz, are:

1. The bills should be *understandable by the recipient* and expressed in non-DP terminology

2. The bills should be *repeatable and comparable* on a year-to-year basis

3. Charges should be *associated with familiar activities*

4. The recipients should be able to compare the bill to their annual budget, business plans, and annual forecasts

5. The bills should charge only for items the user can *control*

6. The bills should help the recipient to establish a *cost/benefit comparison* allowing a measure of the effectiveness of the application

The capacity planner will often be involved in the determination of usage, operating system overhead, control program overhead, indirect usage costs, and forecasted usage. A typical unit cost calculation for resource accounting is:

$$\text{Unit Cost} = \frac{\text{Total Cost}}{\text{Total Usage}} \tag{9}$$

Gewurtz points out that costing by actual usage creates several problems for chargeback accounting. The units billed will vary and are unknown until the end of the billing period. There will be no consistency among billing periods and the process cannot be used to control budgets. Thus, it recovers the total costs of resources but is undesirable for billing.

The usage of the resources by the application may consist of several components. For example:

$$\text{Application Usage Cost} = \begin{bmatrix} \text{Operating System Overhead} \\ + \\ \text{Control Program Overhead} \\ + \\ \text{Indirect Usage Cost} \end{bmatrix} \tag{10}$$

In addition, the environment of today's computer systems provides numerous complicating factors, such as multiprogramming, virtual storage, priority processing, shift differentials, and multiprocessors (often in combination with multiple system images, partitions, or domains). The complexity and cost of chargeback itself can easily become unmanageable.

An alternative to costing by actual usage, sometimes considered in order to stabilize unit costs, is costing by practical capacity. *Practical capacity* is the maximum usage that can be processed on a particular resource at an acceptable level of performance. The unit cost is very stable when based on practical capacity, says Gewurtz, but it will not recover the total cost of the resource unless the users use 100 percent of the practical capacity. This is not operationally desirable, for a variety of reasons; however, this method can determine the cost of retaining excess capacity, since it is independent of actual or projected usage.

The next option for costing is costing by projected usage. The advantage of this approach is that resource accounting is integrated with MIS budgeting. The annual expense of each resource is divided by the annual projected usage:

$$\text{Unit Cost} = \frac{\text{Forecasted Cost}}{\text{Forecasted Usage}}$$

The result is a stable unit billing rate for the year. This is a very common technique used by major MIS environments. It can be used by the billed recipients to predict and control their budgets. A problem with this approach, according to Gewurtz, is that if projected usage is low, costs will be high and thus discourage users (also, the opposite is true). This approach does not equitably charge for new systems technology where "pioneer" users absorb the total costs. In the case of initial excess capacity for new technology, costs are usually recovered based on long-term forecasts, whereas short-term costs are recovered by the total organization.

Natural unit billing establishes a fixed billing rate for each billing unit (for example, an on-line transaction or a payroll check). Workload characterization techniques are employed to group resource profiles for natural units. For batch systems, these groups may be defined in terms of output (for example, check processed, customer invoices, reports, etc.). This method can result in a large number of billing rates and can require a very complex resource accounting system. Rates must be frequently adjusted in order to capture the costs of correlated system resources. The advantages to this methodology are numerous, both for the users and the capacity planner. It is well understood by the users and can be used for forecasting future load, controlling usage and budgeting, and determining the value of MIS processing budgets. The problem with this approach is that there may be too much variability within the resource usage categories to establish "typical" values. Thus, adjustments may be numerous for users who have highly unpredictable workloads.

The last, and least frequently used, approach to billing is the *fixed price annual contract*. Gewurtz recommends this for users who have a well-understood and predictable workload. With accurate load forecasts, this approach can be an extremely simple chargeback process and is easy to understand and operate.

Hoffman and Fuerst [4], emphasize the need of chargeback to provide control of costs, establish accountability, and, like Gewurtz, provide a basis for decision making. Once a base of historical information is established for costs, it is then possible to estimate future costs. Users can justify their level of spending by being made accountable to a certain level of usage. MIS is likewise made accountable by providing service at a desired level and specified cost. Longer-term planning and commitments are possible, and the cost benefits to alternative IS sources (such as end-user computing, departmental, PC-LANs, client/server, etc.) can be evaluated.

It is not surprising that after an effective chargeback and cost control system is implemented, substantial organizational changes may take place. Changes may include improvements in decision making regarding the priority of MIS workloads, decisions regarding out-sourcing, mergers, data center consolidations, downsizing, rightsizing and the actual dollar value of the application workloads. Given the mission-critical applications and the cost of running them, the need (or lack thereof) of disaster recovery capabilities (business continuity services) may be established. With cost measurements in place, the executive ranks of management have a clearer picture of the value of MIS and the services and benefits performed.

3.6 REFERENCES

1. Browning, Tim. "Forecasting Computer Resources Using Business Elements: A Pilot Study." *CMG Conference Proceedings*, 1990, pp. 421–427.

2. Rosenberg, Jerry. L. "Financial Considerations in Capacity Planning." *CMG Conference Proceedings*, 1987, pp. 531–535.

3. Gewurtz, G. "Chargeback Concepts." *CMG Conference Proceedings*, 1988, pp. 617–619.

4. Hoffman, F. W. and W. L. Fuerst. "Designing and Using Chargeback Systems: A Tutorial." *CMG Conference Proceedings*, 1985, pp. 586–588.

4

Forecasting, Predictions, and Planning

What's past, and what's to come, is strew'd with husks
And formless ruin of oblivion.

— William Shakespeare, *Troilus and Cressida*

4.1 PLANNING VS. FORECASTING

Since ancient times man has sought out the means to foretell the future. Often, those who claim to be able to predict future events invoke mysterious and magical technologies such as astrology, magical diagrams and formulae, altered states of consciousness, etc. In the classical western traditions of learning, the prophetic soothsayer ranges from the divine to the debased.

Men (and women) of means, when facing momentous and uncertain decision points in their lives, will inevitably turn to those who claim to be able to predict the future. Literature and philosophy often explores the conceptual tension between a future "created" by informed agents of change versus a future of destiny, fate, and compelling forces willed by the gods or less personal forces. Modern corporate executives, like tribal leaders, kings, and heads of state from the past, must plan for the future. Twentieth century business planning is an inherently "creation-centered" process in which the future is not merely "prepared for," like getting out the umbrella in anticipation of an oncoming rainstorm, but also "shaped," or brought about, by willful manipulation of events. In this respect, strange as it may seem, the modern business planner reflects the epistemology of the shaman-magician-alchemist who also attempts to invoke new realities by will. Of course, a big difference between the two is the metaphysics of contemporary science. Events are described in terms of causality, probability, or in terms of mathematical risk. Modern project planning methodologies and their associated milestones and task decompostions, still resemble, at least in form, the recipe-like formulations of the pre-scientific magus. The conceptual framework, however, is thoroughly "modern." The rise of information technology has brought with it a notable shift in conceptual paradigms, from the mechanistic world view of Newton and Descartes, to a systemic world view in which we are embedded in nature-as-information-system. Analytic modeling and neural network computing has surfaced the real need to view people, computers and enterprise as interdependent systems within systems.

Unlike the mystics of new age and occult traditions, the capacity planner is bound to this world by his craft. The craft holds him to the world and the mystic goes off through his psyche into the transcendent. It would be very surprising indeed for a corporate executive to employ a mystic. The primary reason for this is the need by managers to exercise control over the process of business planning. An epistemology that aims relentlessly at control rules out the possibility of transcendence.

Planning is inextricably intertwined with forecasting. Periodic forecasts help the planning process reassess its direction toward a goal, just as planning gives focus and direction to the forecasting process. Planning without forecasting is futile; forecasting in the absence of a plan is blind.

The capacity planner is expected to be able to forecast based on reasonable assumptions and an analysis of current and historical patterns. The mathematically sophisticated analyses performed for the purpose of statistical forecasting are in sharp contrast to the recipe-outline approach of project management planning methodologies. Whereas analytical forecasting techniques are generally quantitative and focus on identifying patterns in data that "influence" the future, project planning tends to be highly conceptual and focused on the causal sequence of events, which results in achieving some goal. The goal is achieved in the future (if it is achievable at all), and the steps toward that goal are continuously monitored. As the project moves forward, the goal may become more clearly possible or impossible. The capacity planning function, as a kind of resource navigator, can play an evaluative role by providing reiterative and periodic reassessment of the current and expected capacity of resources required to meet the plan. As

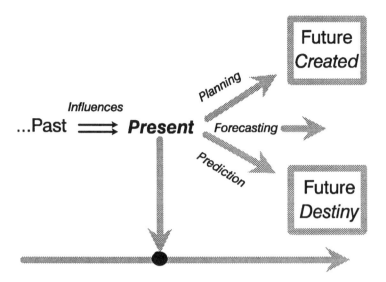

Figure 4.1 Prediction, planning, and forecasting—the future as destiny and creation

time goes by, and more information is available, the application of forecasting techniques becomes more (or less) useful. A critical assumption in forecasting is that the system being forecast has sufficient past behavior (*sufficient* meaning a past record of data at least equal in time span from the present as the future time period being predicted) to exhibit patterns of variation that model the conditions expected in the future.

It is not unusual that the causal factors influencing the past behaviors are either unknown or only partially known. In very complex computer systems, thorough analytic modeling, even of a peripheral I/O subsystem, may be too intricate and/or too expensive. The greater the complexity of any system whose behavior we are trying to predict, the more expensive will be the expenditure of resources for analysis. What is often needed is a reasonable estimate or guess about future conditions. What is reasonable? That will depend on the risk that is comfortable for the risk taker—usually, some measure of the probability of error in the forecast can be specified and evaluated in the light of many competing alternative scenarios—and the cost of reducing uncertainty by "expensive" forecasting techniques.

Making critical decisions in the face of great uncertainty and risk—very well known to the corporate manager—can be a blend of art and science. How do we advise management on what decisions to make? What are the decision support options? In the lack of certainty there is also opportunity—

the opportunity to make a reasonable or fortunate guess. What we need is an "educated" guess—a guess that has some probability of being right based on the facts at hand (a "factualized" guess). On the other hand, if the facts at hand are not analytically tractable, i.e., are not useful for developing inferences predicated on some measurements, then a non-empirical methodology will most likely be employed, such as intuition, judgment, logic, etc. A good example of a nonempirical approach is the use of a "prediction" by an "expert" (or someone who has a good reputation with management for making a good guess).

Critics may discredit past information and techniques, which rely on the projection of past patterns into the future, if there are no clear grounds for a causal relationship. There may be the belief that there is no relationship between past and current or future states of a computer system, i.e., that the past does not "cause" the "future" or even the "present." Nevertheless, it is often important to be able to describe the general tendency of behavior over time and to look for cycles (seasonality) or response patterns to some periodic and reoccurring phenomena, either outside or inside the system. The repetitive and sequential groupings of events, whether viewed as the events constantly conjoined by habit of mind or as the perception of some external property of the world, is a basis for causal thinking. Early twentieth century thinking has demonstrated the practicality of causal models (and its limitations).

4.2 STATISTICAL FORECASTING

As we venture out upon the road of systems forecasting, the horizon of certainty recedes before us like a misty cloud of probabilities. Statistical forecasting is both a very exacting discipline and a treacherous one to those unskilled in its intricacies. Given sufficient history and a clear definition of variables, the statistical model can be superbly useful. Although the rules are quite specific for any given statistical procedure, the application of one model over another may require the wisdom of substantial experience.

The focus of this book will not be so much on what statistics is nor how statistics is used in general, but how statistics is best used in the activities of capacity planning. There are many fine books and college courses on statistics. The capacity planner is almost always confronted with two extremes regarding the use of statistics. On the one hand, some statistical techniques are so elaborate and mathematically sophisticated that they are incomprehensible to the nonstatistician or, even if comprehensible to the analyst, bewildering to the decision-makers on whose behalf the analysis was made. The other extreme is that the technique is so common (for example, taking the average of several numbers) that one is lulled into applying the technique inappropriately (for example, using the arithmetic mean when the geometric or harmonic mean is appropriate).

Just as "information" may be extracted from a collection of data, so too may predictive patterns be revealed in a collection of time series data. The search for patterns which reveal information about the relationships between resource usage, time, and/or business elements outside the conceptual boundaries of computer systems architecture, is fundamental to both causal and statistical models. Predictive information is essential for planning and the evaluation of scenarios which constitute the decision space of the system administrator/manager.

4.3 PROBABILITY AND THE ANALYSIS OF RISK

What is the risk of plan A versus plan B? What if I don't upgrade the computer resource, given its past rate of consumption, by a certain date? How likely is it that the forecast is accurate? What will be the predictive accuracy of our model? All of these questions are addressed by the science of decision making via the discipline of mathematical probability and hypothesis testing. In a prediction exercise, our best estimaters of what some parameter will be are always relative to the probabilities of its occurrence relative to all other alternatives.

One way to say how accurate an estimate is, is to surround the estimate with a confidence interval, also called an error bound. This is the plus or minus part of an expression, such as: The value of such and such is 100 *plus or minus* 10. Here are some examples:

- You have estimated the average disk space utilization for UNIX systems in manufacturing environments nationwide, as X. The survey does not include every installation in the country, so this is just an estimate. However, it is a random sample. Now you want to show how reliable this estimate is.

    First, find the standard deviation of the sample data and multiply it by 1.96. The mean minus two standard deviations is the lower limit of the

95 percent confidence interval. The mean plus two standard deviations is the upper limit of the 95 percent confidence interval. So you can state with 95 percent confidence that the true average disk space utilization lies in this interval. The confidence level in this case is 95 percent.

- You are using regression to predict the number of scratch tape mounts per day on the basis of application natural unit volumes for the previous day. Suppose that there were X natural units today, and your model predicts 320 tape mounts tomorrow, with a standard deviation of 42 tape mounts. The 95 percent confidence interval is 320 ± 42 or 278 to 362 tapes.

  What this means is the following: On 95 percent of all days that follow a day with X natural units, you can expect to mount somewhere between 278 and 362 scratch tapes. The upper limit of confidence is 362. This is the number of tapes you need to have if you want to be 95 percent certain of not running out.

The *interval forecast* is embedded within the context of confidence limits as compared to the *point forecast.* The point forecast is usually reported to management and the accuracy of the forecast is then assessed relative to the actual measurements. Unfortunately, not many managers have statistical sophistication to appreciate the confidence limit; however, once explained, it becomes a useful decision boundary for determining the risks associated with the point forecast.

In strict mathematical terminology, the confidence limit, when used in linear regression, is called the prediction interval. Given a regression equation of the form:

$$y = b_0 + b_1 x$$

the prediction is defined as:

$$y \pm t_{n-2, 1-\alpha/2} \; S_{y|x} \sqrt{\frac{1}{q} + \frac{1}{n} + \frac{x_0 - \overline{x}^2}{(n-1)S_x^2}}$$

where

n = the number of points used in the calculation
q = the number of points to be estimated

$t_{n-2, 1-\alpha/2}$ is the $100(1-\alpha)\%$ point on the t distribution with $n-2$ degrees of freedom and

$$S_{y|x} = \sqrt{\frac{(n-1)}{(n-2)} S_y^2 - b_1^2 S_x^2}$$

There are many forecasting techniques which will compute interval forecasts ([1], [2], [3]). They include stepwise autoregression, exponential smoothing, Holt-Winters, Box-Jenkins, statespace, and X11. These techniques vary by time and skill of the user and the quality of the forecasts depend much on the quality of the historical data.

4.4 CONTINGENCY—SYSTEM FAILURE AND RECOVERY

The capacity planner is often an integral player in the areas of disaster recovery planning and testing. What is the minimum capacity of a recovery environment? What are the resource requirements of enterprise-critical applications? How much disk space, scratch tapes, communications bandwidth, etc., do we need to recover a computer system? The capacity planner should, if involved with *capacity management,* be able to provide a summary description, at some high level of planning, of all workloads and systems.

If multiple systems with varying configurations (different real or expanded memory storage, different I/O capacities, etc.) are to be recovered, the capacity planner will most likely use *normalization* techniques to assess the resource profiles of multiple workloads relative to some common scale. Normalization is typically used in cost accounting and chargeback disciplines where the cost of running a workload can be equalized (despite performance differences, such as execution time) across multiple systems (for example, in a shared spool environment where jobs arrive from a central point but may be dispatched on multiple computers or multiple operating system images within the same complex).

The capacity profile of recoverable workloads determines the cost of disaster recovery configurations. The decision of management as to how much risk is acceptable relative to the cost of providing recovery capacity is usually based on the probability of a disaster and the cost impact of the disaster. For out-sourced environments, there may be expensive penalties to the outsourcer if service is not provided within some specific interval. Given the reliability of system components, and availability and ability to replace these components, a component failure impact analysis may be performed to identify "disasters" that can arise solely due to failure of internal system components. If alternative resources are available, for example, a slower CPU or memory constrained system, analytic modeling may be used to predict the impact to service.

4.5 PREDICTION, FORECASTING, AND VISUALIZATION

In capacity planning, the horizon of being is time. Time is the limiting factor which circumscribes the present and gives boundaries to possibilities. Time is the continuum or background field for the event space variables of time series analysis. The use of visual language structures describe relationships between events with time as a continuum. Even in ancient times, the eternal quality of the Now was symbolized visually using mandalas and similar symbols. The mandala of capacity planning is statistical graphics—a union of equation and geometry. Like the mandala, statistical graphics can represent patterns of change over time visually demonstrating the form of change as a kind of conclusion or whole. When viewed by those trained in its symbolism, the statistical graphic can sway the mind toward an image of some future possibility.

The analytical task of capacity forecasting is the generation of inductive inferences or sets of statistically disciplined extrapolations or projections. The results of the analysis should isolate "ranges" within which specific parametric or coefficient values are expected to fall. The appropriate instrument for this type of analysis paradigm is the use of a Bayesian process whereby subjective probabilities are gradually transformed into objective indices, such that a range of alternatives—all belonging to the same qualitative set—is generated.

The perception and understanding of the future as the realization of a plan, the result of past influences or the outcome of both, may be divided into the factual (the knowledge expressed in words and numbers) and the emotional (the knowledge perceived in images and feelings). Too often the capacity planner fails to communicate to management the appropriate images. Images (or graphics) must not distort, but fully portray the important decision support information. Graphics, discussion, and the feelings which arise from them contribute to the motivational energy of managerial action. Busy managers are primarily focused on visual and auditory activities. Few have time to read. A capacity study which indicates a need to take some non-trivial action, such as system reconfiguration or the purchase of expensive computer resources, must communicate in such a way that feelings of urgency are aroused. Factual knowledge without feelings is impotent to effect change.

4.6 REFERENCES

1. Chatfield, C., *The Analysis of Times Series: An Introduction*, 2nd ed., London, Chapman and Hall, 1980.

2. Harvey, A. C., *The Economic Analysis of Time Series*, Oxford, Philip Allan, 1981.

3. Ingraham, B. A., "Introduction to Box-Jenkins Forecasting," *CMG'86 Conference Proceedings*, The Computer Measurement Group, 1986.

5

Statistical Forecasting for Capacity Planning

5.1 TRENDS AND PATTERNS OF ACTIVITY

Statistical forecasting activities are basically focused on identifying patterns in historical data that can be mathematically extended into future time periods. Ideally, the predictor variable or variables can be directly related to some natural unit of activity within the enterprise. For time-series regression, the passage of time itself is used as the predictor variable. Most often, time-series regression is used to perform data smoothing and provide a graphic picture of the general trend of a data series.

In order to understand a data series it is important to classify the series according to certain basic fundamental time-oriented distribution topologies. The advantage of this process is that mathematical algorithms are available to extend the series into future states based upon the natural patterns operative in the past.

Data values may have any of four basic patterns: *cyclical, trending, lumpy,* or *horizontal.* The series of data values may also show a combination of these patterns.

The examination of historical data may reveal regularly recurring increases and decreases in resource usage at certain times of the year. This *cyclic* pattern of data values is also called *seasonality.* The data fluctuate according to a predictable pattern. There are also longer cycles, lasting several years or decades, but these are not very useful to capacity planners. It is rare that the commercial world would plan decades in advance.

The following criteria may be used to classify a series of data as *seasonal:*

- There should be some reason for the peak time period (e.g., Christmas buying for retailers, Mother's Day long-distance calling for telephone companies, etc.)

- The peak time period must be significantly higher than during the rest of the year

- The pattern should repeat over several years

- The peak period must be in the same season every year, i.e., it must be predictable

If the pattern of data shows a gradual increase or decrease over time, the data are considered to show a *trend.* Usually, this can be identified with regression analysis (linear or nonlinear, multiple or simple). This is the most common (and probably most abused) method for trend analysis. Simple regression techniques reveal trend only. They are limited by the reality that *only* the past is used in the analysis.

Lumpy distributions are characterized by a lot of variation without an overall direction or trend. Time-series regression analysis may be flat in this case. Some mathematicians might opt for a causal modeling approach in this situation, such as field dynamic modeling, in order to forecast future states of a turbulent "field" of vectors. However, causal modeling assumes that you know what may be influencing the pattern and that you also have a history of these factors over the same time intervals.

Horizontal data tend to have a constant average value despite variation within the individual data values. There is not much change from one forecast interval to the next. Because of the near constant average values, this distribution is also called stationary or flat. If the distribution has little fluctuation, it is said to be not lumpy, and time-series regression can be used.

Most common to capacity planners is the *trend-seasonal* patterns in which both a trend and seasonality are combined. These distributions are either additive, i.e., the peaks are at about the same height with the respect to the trend line, or multiplicative, i.e., the peaks get bigger over the trend line. Figures 5.1 through 5.6 show some ideal trend-seasonal patterns. Typical mathematical representation for trend-seasonal patterns:

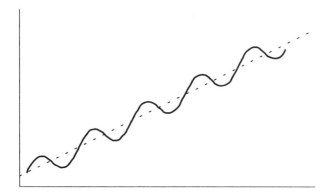

Figure 5.1 Additive seasonality—increasing linear trend

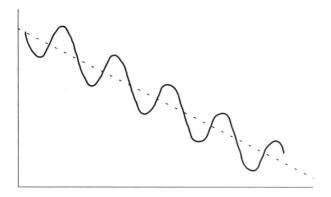

Figure 5.2 Additive seasonality—decreasing linear trend

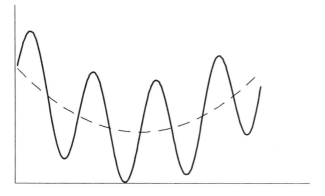

Figure 5.3 Additive seasonality—changing linear trend

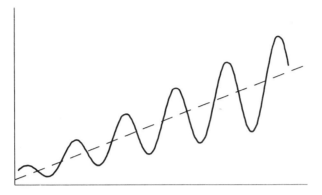

Figure 5.4 Multiplicative seasonality—increasing linear trend

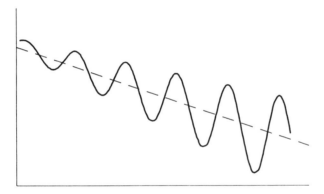

Figure 5.5 Multiplicative seasonality—decreasing linear trend

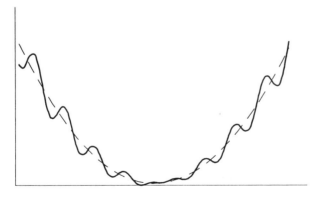

Figure 5.6 Multiplicative seasonality—changing trend

The *additive cyclical series with increasing linear trend* could be represented using the sine function (for cyclical characteristics) and the linear function:

$$f(x) = \sin(x) + (a + bx) \tag{1}$$

The *additive cyclical series with decreasing linear trend* could be represented in a similar fashion as:

$$f(x) = \sin(x) - (a + bx) \tag{2}$$

The *additive cyclical series with changing trend,* e.g., parabolic, could be represented as:

$$f(x) = \sin(x) - (a + bx + cx^2) \tag{3}$$

The *multiplicative cyclical series with increasing or decreasing linear trend* could be represented as:

$$f(x) = \sin(x)(a + bx) \tag{4}$$

The *multiplicative cyclical series with changing trend,* again using the parabolic curve, can be represented as:

$$f(x) = \sin(x)(a + bx + cx^2) \tag{5}$$

5.2 REGRESSION TECHNIQUES FOR CAPACITY PLANNING

There are many fine statistics books on the subject of linear regression. The emphasis in this book will be focused on the application of linear regression to capacity planning activities in a business context.

Capacity planning uses two general categories of regression techniques:

1. Time-series Models—used to forecast time-series data, i.e., a series of values for some variable as measured at equally space points in time, and

2   Causal Models—used to forecast data in which the predictor variable(s) represents something other than time. Natural forecasting unit techniques use this approach. For an example, see Section 5.3.

The assumption of time-series forecasting is that today is like yesterday and tomorrow or that the best predictor of the future is the past. Sometimes this seems to be true. Other times it is only wishful thinking to presume that one can "uncover" a hidden linear trend in an otherwise scattered set of points. If a distribution is truly linear (i.e., in the sense of a line), then a graph will suffice (even without connecting the dots) to portray this property. It is when the distribution is *somewhat* linear that time-series models help illuminate (or create) the "hidden" line. Time series is also called "straight-line projection." Capacity planners use simple (one variable) linear regression frequently when examining the trend of only one predictor variable. It is assumed that the response must be a linear function of the predictor.

Consider the illustration of the time-series regression in Figure 5.7. Here the r-square value (coefficient of determination) is very low. The time-series linear model is clearly inappropriate. However, a linear regression causal model may turn out to be a good fit. For example, in Figure 5.8, the use of a natural forecasting unit for the regression model yields a much closer fit to the actual resource units. Furthermore, it also illustrates that linear models need not involve straight lines.

If one is willing to investigate the use of nonlinear (or curvilinear) techniques, it is possible, given some justifications based on the expected properties of the data distribution, to improve linear regression models in terms of fit to the actual data (see Figure 5.9). In this example, a quadratic time-series is contrasted with other models. In this case, time is used as a quadratic function.

Despite the improvement by using causal factors in the regression model, it can be interesting without being useful. Unless you can predict the future

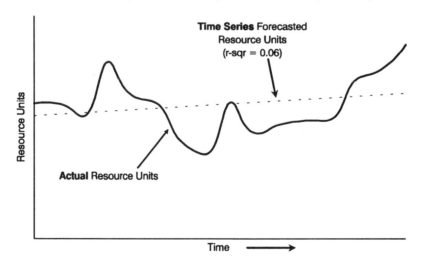

Figure 5.7 Comparison of actual resource units for time-series forecast

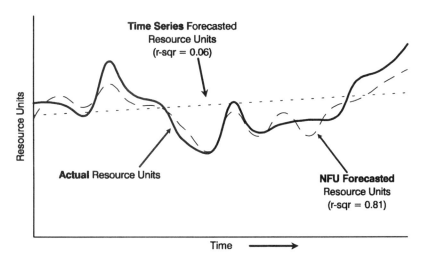

Figure 5.8 Comparison of time-series and NFU regression models

values of the *causal* variables with a reasonable degree of accuracy, your model is of little value. In addition, one must determine which factors—such as business volume, sales, housing starts, socioeconomic factors—are likely to be good predictors of the dependent variable of interest.

Capacity planners find that simple linear strategies are seldom effective in the real world of complex systems. Linear regression, as a future-building

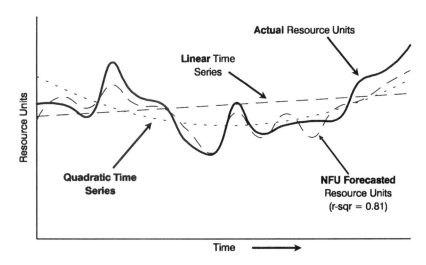

Figure 5.9 Comparison of linear time series, NFU model, and quadratic time series

methodology, has certain limitations. Some of these limitations have been mentioned, but we will summarize them here:

- Linear regression is of little use unless there is a measurable trend in the data.

- The trend must be linear. The line that best fits the data should be a straight line. If this is not the case, the analyst must transform the data to make it linear.

- Linear regression is not effective unless you have a reasonable amount of data.

- The response values must be independent of one another; if this is not true, then the model appears to be significant but isn't.

- Linear regression, like other forecast methods, cannot be used to predict values very far in the future.

Despite these limitations, the reader will find that linear regression dominates the world of capacity planning, as demonstrated by numerous presentations and articles that use or abuse this technique. Probably the best reason for this is that it is a simple and understandable technique, which often yields comparable results achieved by more complex models that people do not understand.

5.3   WEIGHTED LINEAR REGRESSION—A PREFERENCE FOR THE RECENT PAST

It is not uncommon in regression forecasting that the resource being studied is driven by a changing workload. For example, if an application workload is undergoing constant maintenance (as is usually the case), then recent data regarding resource usage is more valuable than older data. Standard linear regression techniques give equal value to all past data. That can be a problem. One solution is to improve the accuracy of forecasts by modifying the regression models to give recent data more weight—hence, *weighted* linear regression. The weights decline from recent data to older data, and the regression line fits later data points more closely than the standard approach; it better reflects the changes in the workload.

To illustrate weighted linear regression, I used actual data provided by a credit bureau. The company needed to predict the CPU hours that would be required in the last quarter of 1992. Long experience has shown that CPU hours in a given quarter are closely related to certain business factors (predictor variable) from the previous quarter. The business factor is also called the Natural Forecasting Unit (NFU).

Figure 5.10 demonstrates this correlation. Moving to the right on the chart, from lower to higher values of the predictor variable, the points are generally higher, meaning that the CPU hours become greater.

The graph's horizontal axis represents associated business factor. Notice that the points indicate a slight slowdown in the increase in CPU hours relative to the predictor variable. The slowdown accompanies changes in the application workload the company made during the measurement intervals.

If the values from a regression analysis are plotted on the graph, the position of the line's right end point is the predicted number of CPU hours.

The problem with using the standard linear regression model here is that the line fits the early data points more closely than it fits the later ones. What is needed is a set of weights, which decline from recent data, to older data so that the prediction for recent data is lower than the standard prediction.

To do this, you use the weights themselves and the predictor variables multiplied by the weights as the X range, and you use the CPU hours multiplied by the weights as the Y range with an intercept of zero. You compute

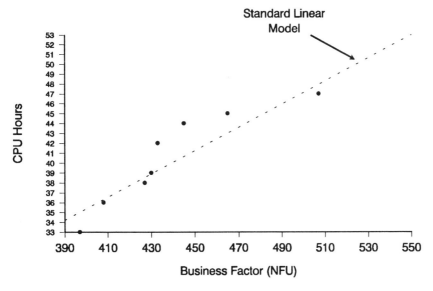

Figure 5.10 Data show the scattergram between the business factors and CPU hours. The dashed line, which predicts CPU hours for the next quarter, is based on the standard regression model.

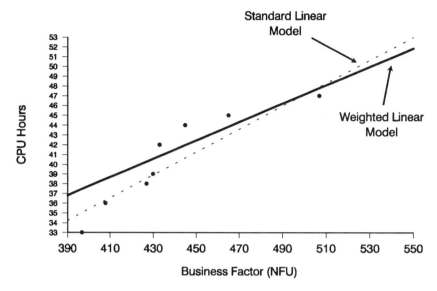

Figure 5.11 Standard and weighted linear models

predicted CPU hours by multiplying each business factor value by the second *X* coefficient and adding that product to the first *X* coefficient. The estimated parameters obtained by this method are those that minimize the weighted residual sum of squares:

$$\sum w_i \, (y_i - \beta_0 - \beta_1 x_1 - \cdots \beta_m x_m)^2$$

The solid line in Figure 5.11, labeled *weighted linear model*, fits later data points more closely than the broken line, and it better reflects the changes in business factors. As you can see from the figure, the discounted prediction for recent data is lower than the standard prediction for the same period.

5.3.1 Computing the Weights

A generally successful method for computing the weights is by taking the square root of the discount factor and raising it to the power indicated by the reverse ordinal rank of the data value over time. For example, if you have five data items, the calculations, using a 0.70 discount factor, would be as shown in Table 5.1.

Table 5.1 Calculating Weights for Five Data Items

Reverse Ordinal Rank	Calculation	Weight
5	$(\sqrt{0.70})^5$	0.41
4	$(\sqrt{0.70})^4$	0.49
3	$(\sqrt{0.70})^3$	0.59
2	$(\sqrt{0.70})^2$	0.70
1	$(\sqrt{0.70})^1$	0.84
0	$(\sqrt{0.70})^0$	1.00

Because a number between 0 and 1 is made smaller by being raised to a higher power, the results increase as the values in time decrease. When the discount factor is 1.00, all data get equal weight and the results are the same as with the standard approach. Table 5.2 shows the four sets of weights you get by using four different discount factors.

How do you choose the best discount factor? This is a matter of judgment and becomes easier with experience. Most capacity planners avoid carrying discounting too far and use modest values: 0.7, 0.8, or 0.9. In this example, I used 0.70 due to the dramatic growth; it also produces a regression line that falls closest to the last data point.

Some more complex data patterns may be difficult to detect on a graph, especially when there is more than one set of X variables. When there is no

Table 5.2 Four Sets of Weights with Discount Factors

Reverse Ordinal Rank	0.70	0.80	0.90	1.00
7	0.29	0.46	0.69	1.00
6	0.34	0.51	0.73	1.00
5	0.41	0.57	0.77	1.00
4	0.49	0.64	0.81	1.00
3	0.59	0.72	0.85	1.00
2	0.70	0.80	0.90	1.00
1	0.84	0.89	0.95	1.00
0	1.00	1.00	1.00	1.00

evidence of changing growth, use a conservative discount factor of 0.90 to avoid unforeseen problems later.

5.4   COMPLEX REGRESSION COMBINATIONS

It is sometimes appropriate to combine several regression techniques in order to create models for environments in which the workload is undergoing frequent change (weighted linear regression) and where monthly forecasts are needed for short term planning (limited reiterative regression). To explore these technique consider the example data in Figure 5.12. This data is the average system utilization for a Tandem 780 CLX system using 8 CPUs operating in pairs. The data is plotted on a weekly basis.

A simple time series regression line would use all of the existing data, with equal weights, and indicate a downward trend. If this approach is used for monthly forecasting, and there has been significant changes to the same workload (e.g., program maintenance, software upgrades, etc.) that could increase future CPU utilization, then the next month's forecast would mis-

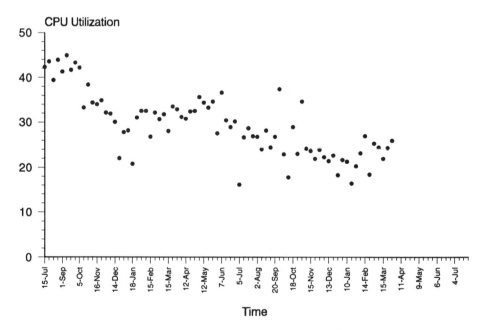

Figure 5.12 Weekly average CPU utilization for Tandem 780

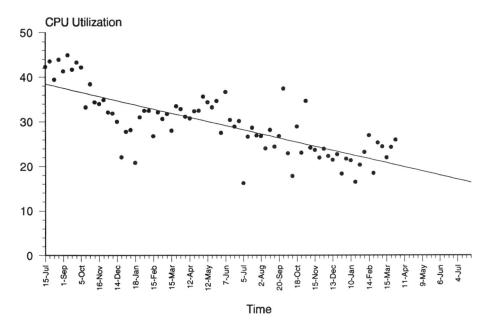

Figure 5.13 CPU data with time-series regression

takenly forecast a lower utilization than the current month. Figure 5.13 shows how a simple time series regression forecast would look.

If the standard time series data and forecast were tracked on a weekly or monthly basis, the mean absolute deviation between the actual measurements and the forecast would be quite large. The mean absolute deviation (MAD) is a method for estimating variation. Although not as good an estimator as the standard deviation, it is easily comprehended by those less inclined to statistical sophistication. You find the absolute value of the difference between each actual measurement and the forecast amount. Then, the mean of these differences is used as an indicator of the variation between forecast and actual. If this value is very high, management's evaluation of the capacity planner's ability to forecast might be correspondingly low. How can the capacity planner provide a more accurate short term forecast?

In the example data, it is known that the environment is volatile due to changes in how the workload responds to drivers. One technique which seems to improve the MAD in this case is to use linear regression over a limited number of past measurements (in this case six measurement intervals were used) and recalculate each month for the new forecast. This ap-

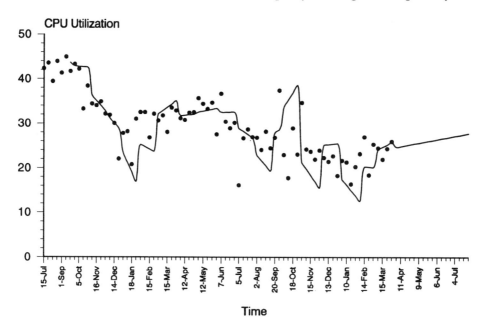

Figure 5.14 Reiterative linear regression forecasting compared to actual

proach means that distant data is totally eliminated (a bold move, perhaps) as new data is included. The effect, when seen graphically, is a much more variable forecast curve which tracks the actual data with a lower MAD. See Figure 5.14.

You will notice that as the forecast is extended considerably beyond the last few actual measurements that this technique then reverts back to a standard linear regression or time-series forecast (in this case an unweighted regression which is based solely on recent data).

This technique works well with short-term forecasts; however, the capacity planner must often produce short- and long-term forecasts. What to do now?

Suppose that one wishes to provide a long-term forecast that doesn't "throw away" the distant past (partial or limited linear regression) and show it in comparison to the short-term forecast model extended over the same future interval? In Figure 5.15, this technique is used to demonstrate the subtle (and not so subtle) shift in magnitude of these two linear regression lines. The dashed line of the weighted linear regression forecast is much more steep, reflecting the upward trend of recent measurements.

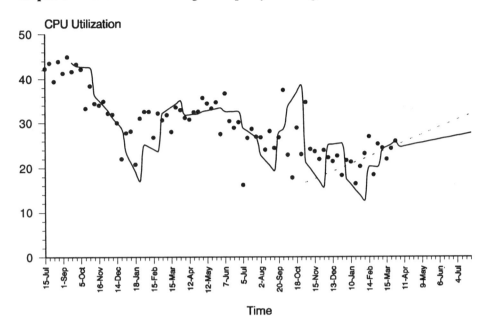

Figure 5.15 Short-term and long-term forecast methods—a comparison

As forecasts are tracked each month, the model may need revision or replacement with other models depending on the measured forecast accuracy, the level of accuracy that is acceptable to management and the level of accuracy that *can* be achieved using the specific modeling technique (confidence intervals).

Short-term forecasting, i.e., routine month-to-month resource forecasting, is of great value to business managers (e.g., sales forecasts) as well as MIS managers. Selecting a short-term forecasting method that is analytically sound can be aided by the following decision chart. However, be mindful that if the situation calls for a certain mathematical procedure, it does not mean that you should disregard human judgement.

5.5 FORECAST MONITORING AND REVISION

Forecasting is somewhat like shooting an arrow at a faraway target under windy conditions. You would like to at least hit the target and hopefully close

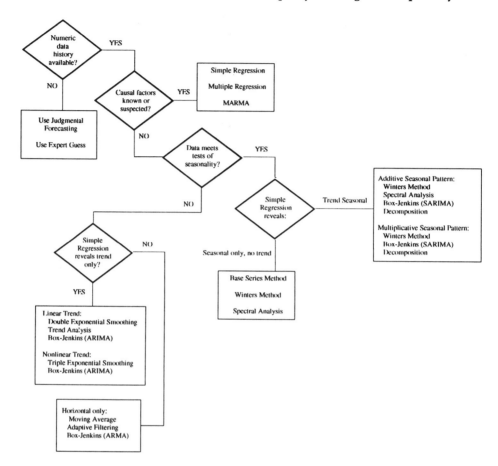

Figure 5.16 Decision points for selecting a short-term forecasting method

to the bull's-eye. It helps, of course, to know which way the wind is blowing (technically called a "tracking signal") and it also helps to have some practice.

There are two important considerations in monitoring and revising forecasts used by capacity planners:

- Is the forecast model doing a "good" job?
- What should be done if it is not.

5.5.1 Testing the New Model

The first stage in the forecasting process at which the accuracy of the model should be checked is at the time the new model is developed. One traditional way of doing this is to ask yourself "If I had been using this model in the past, would it have forecast accurately?". One way to answer this question is to compare the amount of variation in the data explained by the model to the amount of variation that is unexplained and then determine the probability that this value could have resulted from chance alone. You can test a regression model by using ANOVA (analysis of variance). The F value statistic used in ANOVA is the ratio of the amount of variation explained to the amount of variation unexplained. A high F value means the model is doing a good job. But how high should it be? To determine that, a p value (for probability) is determined in order to specify the probability that the F value could have resulted from chance alone. You want the p value to be low; usually, less than 0.05.

5.5.2 Prediction-Realization Diagram

The prediction-realization diagram is a useful graphic device for monitoring forecasts.

This technique is based on the fact that if your forecasts were always 100 percent perfect, and this was drawn on a graph with the forecasts on one axis and the actual values on the other, then the points would form a straight line at a 45-degree angle as demonstrated in Figure 5.17.

The degree to which the actual graph is similar to this ideal graph can be used as a guide to indicate how well the model is doing. The line of perfect forecasts divides the coordinate system into six areas. These areas indicate the magnitude of the six types of forecast error:

- Points in the areas labelled II and V represent errors in predicting turning points, i.e., times when the model predicted an upward trend but produced a downward trend, or vice versa.

- Points in the areas labelled III and IV result when the model correctly predicted a downward trend, but the value was in error or outside an acceptable interval.

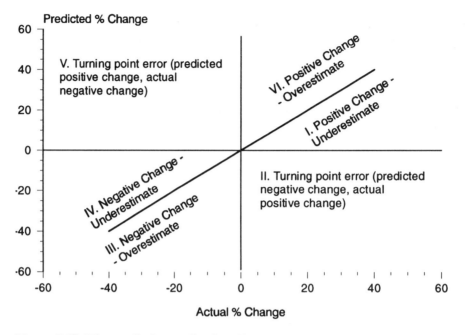

Figure 5.17 The prediction-realization diagram

- Points falling in areas I and VI result when the model corretly predicted an upward trend, but the value was in error or outside an acceptable interval.

5.5.3   Testing a Working Model with Filter Trips and Tracking Signals

Two of the simplest and most common tests for monitoring the performance of a working forecast model are called the *filter* and the *tracking signal*. Many of the forecasting programs for mainframe computers offer one or both of these tests as options. If they are not available on either mainframe or microcomputer, you can do these tests fairly easily on paper or spreadsheets.

The filter is a test that looks at each forecast to see how different it is from the actual data value, once the latter is known. If the forecast is off by more than a specified amount, the result is called a *filter trip* (like tripping an alarm). Then you have a situation that notifies you that the forecast is outside the limits you have set. You might, for example, set the limit at 4 times the value of the mean absolute deviation (MAD). The filter is not tripped unless the forecast falls outside a 99.8 percent confidence interval around the value.

As an example, suppose the January forecast for tape mounts is 103,000. The actual utilization in January turns out to be 220,000. We can see immediately that the forecast is wrong. The purpose of the demand filter is to warn us whether the forecast is *wrong enough* to make us question the validity of the model we are using.

In this example, the value of MAD that we have calculated, based on (for example) three years of history, is 10,000. Thus, the highest forecast that the demand filter will accept is:

$$220,000 + (4)(10,000) = 260,000$$

and the lowest forecast would be:

$$220,000 - (4)(10,000) = 180,000$$

The forecast, 103,000 is not just wrong, it is *very* wrong. Because it is below the lower limit of 180,000, it is appropriate that the filter trip should flag it as an error.

In a circumstance such as this, the forecaster needs to determine what went wrong. Perhaps that pattern of demand has changed, or a different set of values or assumptions must be utilized. Or possibly it was a one-time event and there isn't any action necessary.

The *tracking signal* is a way of monitoring all the recent forecasts as a group, to see if they are wrong in some consistent way. Using archery as an analogy to forecasting, you might recall that we mentioned wind. The demand for tapes is influenced by many random events that tend to throw the forecast off just as wind tends to deflect arrows in much the same way. If the wind blows consistently in one direction for awhile, and you are aware of it, you can correct for it. This is what the tracking signal enables you to do.

For example, the tracking signal might show that the forecasts tend to be too low every month. It would be possible to adjust the forecast model to prevent this from happening. Perhaps there is an upward trend in tape demand which you are not aware of, or possible you have made an error in the model calculations.

There are two common methods for calculating the tracking signal: the sum of errors and the smoothed error (exponentially smoothed average of

Table 5.3 Critical Values for the Tracking Signal for Various Confidence Levels

Confidence Level	C =0.1	=0.2	=0.3
0.20	3.6	2.6	2.1
0.10	4.7	2.9	2.8
0.05	5.6	4.1	3.5
0.04	5.9	4.3	3.7
0.03	6.3	4.6	3.9
0.02	6.8	5.0	4.3
0.01	7.5	5.6	4.9

past errors). Here, error means the difference between the forecast and the actual data value for any given time interval.

For capacity planning purposes, the sum of errors method is usually quite effective.

5.5.4 Sum of Errors Method

In this method for calculating the tracking signal, one just adds up all the error terms and divides by the smoothed MAD (mean absolute deviation). In other words, at the end of each forecast period you add the latest forecast error to a running total of all the errors. Then you update the value of MAD by exponential smoothing. Finally, you get the ratio of the two. This ratio is the tracking signal.

$$\text{Tracking Signal} = \frac{\left| \sum (y - y) \right|}{\sum |y - y|/n}$$

The tracking signal should be low, because the sum of the forecast errors should be close to zero. If the forecast is too high about as often as it is too low, half of the errors will be positive and the other half will be negative, and they should cancel each other out.

To test the tracking signal to see if it a problem with the forecast, you see if it exceeds a critical value C. The C value is set according to the confidence level desired, as shown in Table 5.3.

5.5.5 Summary of Forecast Monitoring

A forecasting model should be evaluated periodically, both during the development stage and after the model is in use. Some of the most common testing methods include the analysis of variance (ANOVA), the correlation coefficient, the filter, and the tracking signal. Graphic methods for monitoring forecast performance include the prediction-realization diagram and/or graphical comparison of actual to forecast.

6

Capacity Planning and Systems Optimization

6.1 APPLICATIONS

There are numerous applications of statistical methods to both computer performance management and capacity planning. The following study, conducted in a large MVS mainframe environment in the spring of 1993, demonstrates how these techniques can be effective in the areas of problem analysis, systems optimization, and the capacity of system queuing properties.

6.1.1 Example System Optimization Study for Batch Workloads

A challenging technical analysis was performed, which made use of linear regression techniques, of two MVS system domains running under the Amdahl Multi-Domain Facility. These systems were designated with system IDs of SYSTEM 1 and SYSTEM 2. The objectives of the study were to determine the optimum number of *batch initiators* (which provide pathways into the system for batch work) and *job classes* (which categorize the type of work to be processed). Linear regression was used to predict the optimum processing performance relative to the number of active batch initiators. Statistical cluster analysis was used to develop job class structures by exploiting the natural patterns of resource requirements in the workload. The final results indicated that SYSTEM 1 should have 14 batch initiators and SYSTEM 2 should have 16 initiators. These systems had more than this number of initiators at the time of the project. The effect of having too many initiators (in MVS called "over-initiation") is that the overall batch workload runs slower when all initiators are active (due to contention for the CPU). On the other hand, the effect of having too few initiators would be that jobs wait to execute and this also lowers throughput.

The optimum job class assignments that were derived from the study are based on three resource limited classes and two operational categories for a total of six classes. This classification of the workload will optimize the categorization of work such that (1) a large number of jobs may be completed in a short time, and (2) job scheduling will be simplified, since each class represents a homogeneous set of jobs. The previous job class structure was needlessly complex by including overlapping, redundant, or seldom-used job classes.

In order to improve batch throughput and reduce wait times, management desired answers to the following questions:

- How many job initiators should we have on each system, i.e., what is the optimum number of initiators for each system?

- How many job classes should we have?

- How should the job classes be assigned to the initiators?

Other suggestions from management were:

- Use data from the last six months to determine patterns of usage
- All workload categories have equal priority

6.1.2 Background

These systems were used almost exclusively for batch processing. Over time, many different operational and management initiatives had resulted in a configuration consisting of 35 initiators and 36 job classes.

Categorizing the workload into job classes was based on the similarity of the members of each job class. These similarities were in terms of departmental ownership, application function, and/or resource usage. Past attempts to categorize the workload into priorities of service had been unsuccessful due to the following factors:

1. Priorities changed frequently, based on customer demands, potential for profits, etc.

2. Jobs tended to be unique and nonrepeatable in their resource profiles, i.e., customer-driven requirements were "one time" projects.

3. Until the need for this study was determined, there had been no perceived need for resource-limited job classes.

It was critical to business objectives that service levels be improved for these systems. Work generated from these applications will provide significant profits for the corporation. Improvements in throughput would thus improve customer satisfaction.

6.1.3 Hardware Environment

The mainframe hardware supported multiple operating system images (using the Amdahl Multi-Domain Facility). These domains operated on two separate Amdahl 5990-1400 platforms with different I/O capabilities (due to differences in channel path capacities) and different memory resources (real and expanded storage, see Figure 6.1). These systems shared the same JES spool (for ease of connectivity to printers) and had access to a robotics tape subsystem.

Due to the lack of resource symmetry, workload optimization was analyzed separately for each image. However, given the shared spool environment, jobs could queue for initiation to either system. Thus, the analysis of job class requirements was based on the combined complex.

6.1.4 Software-Initiator Environment

Each operating system image (domain) had a separate initiator specification. The specifications, by class, and the definitions were well documented by the production operations department.

These MVS operating systems had specific performance groups for each job class (as specified in the Installation Performance Specifications parameter list—IEAIPS00 member of SYS1.PARMLIB). All batch processing had the

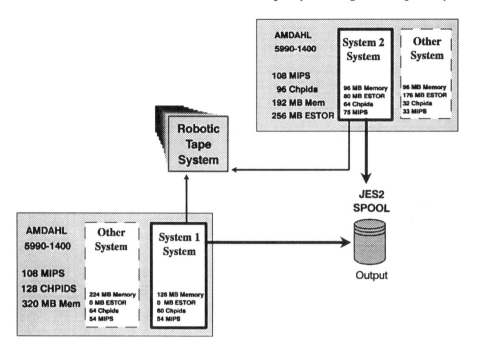

Figure 6.1 Mainframe hardware overview

same performance objectives, i.e., normal batch priority, with the exception of CLASS=H (defined as "Hot Priority" in the standards document) and CLASS=2 (defined in terms of departmental ownership and function—"Department X Jobs. Widget Jobs."). These exceptions operated at a higher priority but with lower domain constraints.

6.1.5 Solutions

The solutions to these problems required the analysis of two different, but related, problems. The first, to determine the optimal number of initiators, involved analyzing the relationship between the total processing time spent on useful (i.e., application program) work and the number of active initiators. Once this was determined, an optimization process was required to determine the maximum value for application program activity relative to variations in the multiprogramming level. The second problem, to determine the types and number of job classes, required the clustering of jobs into patterns based on resource usage. This clustering process can be done using statistical clustering analysis (for resources greater than two) or by graphical analysis (for resources of two or less).

6.1.6 Initiators

Using an SAS-based linear regression analysis and differential calculus (to determine optimal values), the following solutions were proposed:

- The **SYSTEM 1** domain should have **14** initiators. This is the maximum of several statistical analyses ranging from 12–14 initiators, depending on metrics used and extent of data history.

- The **SYSTEM 2** domain should have **16** initiators. This is the maximum of several statistical analyses ranging from 10–16 initiators, depending on metrics used and extent of data history.

Changes to reduce the number of initiators to these levels should result in improved throughput (batch will run faster on the average).

6.1.7 Job Classes

The first step in analyzing the use of job classes was to examine patterns of usage and determine typical values for job frequency by class and resource. An SAS program was written to summarize the total number of jobs by class and to summarize the average wait-time-to-initiate by class. The objective was to see what job classes were experiencing significant waits and what preinitiation resources, if any, were correlated to these waits.

Based on *cluster analysis*, resource-limited job classes were recommended based entirely on tape mounts (or lack thereof). Using tape mounts, print lines, and CPU time resulted in an optimal value of three clusters. This was also the case for CPU time and tape mounts without print line considerations. Finally, eliminating CPU time in the cluster analysis, i.e., a one-resource category analysis, was equivalent to a simple univariate distribution which was grouped using basic descriptive statistics. Approximately 81.36 percent of jobs had zero mounts; 16.81 percent mounted 1–20 tapes; and 0.93 percent mounted more than 20 tapes. However, management wished to add the following additional constraints to job class usage:

- Production jobs should have priority over nonproduction jobs. These jobs should not wait for initiation due to other workloads.

- Production jobs should not share initiators with nonproduction jobs, with the exception of jobs that use tape mounts.

In the processing environment of this study, production jobs were those jobs that were scheduled and submitted by a special production scheduling system used by operations analysts.

Workload isolation was a secondary goal of management by ensuring that production and nonproduction jobs did not directly compete for initiation.

Thus, adding the above additional considerations, there should be six resource-based job classes:

Production-submitted jobs:

- Quick jobs, no tapes   Class=A
- Jobs that mount 1–20 tapes   Class=B
- Jobs that mount >20 tapes   Class=C

Nonproduction submitted jobs:

- Quick jobs, no tapes   Class=D
- Jobs that mount 1–20 tapes   Class=E
- Jobs that mount >20 tapes   Class=F

6.1.8 Initiator Assignments of Job Classes

Initiators should be assigned according to the following guidelines:

- For multiclass initiators, average execution times should be in descending order.

- Define initiators from single to multiclass in increasing order of complexity.

- The number of job class assignments for the lead class should be proportional to the number of jobs expected to run in that class. This proportion may change by shift.

These recommendations are rules of thumb which derive from queueing theory and the optimization of batch performance [1]. An example of an ideal, optimized solution for job class assignments in this case study is demonstrated in Table 6.1. This arrangement assumes that production and non-

Table 6.1 Example of Initiator Job Class Assignments

SYSTEM 1		SYSTEM 2	
Initiator	Class	Initiator	Class
1	A	1	A
2	A	2	A
3	A	3	A
4	C	4	A
5	D	5	A
6	D	6	A
7	D	7	D
8	F	8	D
9	AB	9	D
10	AB	10	D
11	BC	11	D
12	DE	12	D
13	DE	13	B
14	EF	14	E
		15	C
		16	F

production–submitted jobs are equally distributed across resource categories (i.e., equal volume of jobs).

6.1.9 Determining the Optimal Number of Initiators

If batch demand is uniformly increased on a system via the activation of initiators, the total amount of TCB time (CPU time used by the application) increases up to some maximum. Beyond this maximum, the total TCB time declines due to system overhead. Since system functions have priority over application functions when contention occurs for the CPU, it is impossible for a job to complete in less time when it receives less CPU time. This fact results in lower throughput beyond the optimum level of initiation. Thus, optimal initiation will also maximize throughput for a given load level. It is reasonable to assume that the optimal number of initiators will be such that when all available initiators are active, the system is achieving the maximum total TCB time. However, since the resource demands of batch jobs can be quite variable, the optimal initiation point can only be approximated using a statistical averaging approach. Thus, for example, N batch jobs today may use X_1 TCB seconds, while on other days the same number of batch jobs uses X_2 seconds. Over a sufficiently long period of time, we may derive a "typical" or mean value for X,

$$\bar{x} = \frac{\sum\limits_{i=1}^{n} x_i}{n} \tag{1}$$

Using mean values, the optimal number of initiators is therefore defined as the number of initiators that maximizes the mean total TCB time received by the batch initiators. The total amount of TCB time for batch work at a given level of initiation is, *on the average*, the product of the number of active batch initiators and the mean TCB time per initiator, or the mean %TCB time per initiator, for a given interval of time. If x = number of active initiators and $f(x)$ = mean TCB time per initiator, then the estimated total TCB time is $f(x) \bullet x$.

It is desirable to know the *predicted* TCB totals for cases beyond the measured data; for example, the effects of using more or less initiators than currently in use. The optimum value may be less than or greater than current or historical levels.

If a linear equation is fitted to the data using linear regression, the optimum point can be derived. This linear regression model must be able to explain (predict) the variation in TCB time based on the number of active initiators, i.e., the R-SQUARE value should be at least .80 (or 80 percent of the variation in the response variable can be attributed to the linear relation, described in the model, to the predictor variable). Since any error in the regression model will be compounded by the product of the model and the number of active initiators, the R-SQUARE value should be as high as possible. Removal of outliers (if appropriate) and data scaling may help achieve the best fit.

6.1.10 Initiator/TCB Time Data

Prior technical studies [2] suggested using the mean and total of the *percentage* of TCB time as the primary metrics for optimization. In this particular study, the analyst chose the mean and total *proportion* (actual data) in order to avoid nonlinear optimization problems.

An SAS program was coded to analyze the batch TCB time for each corresponding number of active initiators using the following logic:

- Data were read from an MICS database (SCPPGA files) to determine the TCB time for performance groups associated with batch workloads. Data were then summarized, using PROC SUMMARY, on an hourly basis and written to a temporary file. New information was calculated for ALLTCB (the total TCB time) and PCTBAT (the percent of total TCB time) used by batch.

- Data were read from the MICS database (HARCPU files) and sorted by SYSID, YEAR, MONTH, DAY, and HOUR and were then merged with the SCPPGA summary file. The HARCPU file contains information about the number of initiators active (CPUAVB) during the same intervals of time.

- A new variable, DELTA, was defined as PCTBAT/CPUAVB or the *percent* of total TCB time per active initiator. Also defined was BTCBI=BATCH/CPUAVB or the *proportion* of batch TCB time per initiator.

- The merged file was then sorted by SYSID and CPUAVB (number of active initiators).

- PROC MEANS was used to determine the average values per SYSID and number of active initiators (defined as CPUAVB rounded). The results were then printed using PROC PRINT. Several plots were performed to identify the distribution as either somewhat linear or curvilinear.

- Regressions analyses, using PROC SYSREG, were performed using both percent TCB time for batch and proportion of TCB for batch as the predictor variable, i.e., MODEL DELTA=CPUAVB and MODEL BTCBI=CPUAVB. Linear regression equations were derived using the INTERCEPT PARAMETER ESTIMATE and the VARIABLE PARAMETER ESTIMATE in order to determine the linear equation: $y = a + bx$ where a is the intercept and b the coefficient of the predictor variable x. In addition, the R-SQUARE values were compared to determine the percent of variance in the models explained by the linear relationship to the predictor variables. The highest R-SQUARE values determined the model with the best fit.

Table 6.2 SAS Data Table

System ID	Initiators	% Avg TCB per Init	% Total TCB for Batch	Batch TCB per Init	Total TCB for Batch	Total TCB Batch & Other
SYSTEM 1	7	14.18%	99.26%	993.425	6953.98	7005.46
	9	10.99%	98.97%	785.421	7068.79	7141.56
	10	9.89%	98.98%	691.999	6919.99	6990.88
	11	9.00%	99.05%	626.182	6888.01	6953.29
	12	8.26%	99.13%	575.760	6909.12	6969.50
	13	7.62%	99.06%	559.629	7275.17	7342.86
	14	7.07%	99.02%	486.993	6817.90	6885.28
	15	6.58%	98.76%	448.864	6732.96	6816.85
	16	6.17%	98.73%	433.055	6928.88	7017.86
	17	5.81%	98.88%	413.596	7031.13	7110.55
	18	5.48%	98.77%	379.755	6835.59	6919.93
	19	5.22%	99.18%	400.848	7616.11	7679.07

Using SYSTEM 1 as an example, the resulting data can be summarized as shown in Table 6.2.

A plot of the data for batch TCB time per initiator and its associated linear regression line provided a basis for describing the statistical relationship between TCB time and number of active initiators (see Figure 6.2).

The total system TCB time for a given number of initiators is defined as the product of the predicted TCB time (or %TCB time) per initiator (as defined in the linear regression equation) and the number of active initiators (CPUAVB). Thus if $y = a + bx$ is the predicted TCB time (y), then the total TCB time, Z, is defined as

$$z = xy \text{ or } x*(a + bx), \text{ which is } ax + bx^2 \tag{2}$$

This defines a quadratic equation which reaches its maximum at the point where the slope is zero (the crest of the curve). This maximum point can be found using calculus, i.e., the first derivative is set to zero and the equation is then solved for x.

$$z = ax + bx^2$$

$$\frac{dz}{dx} = a + 2bx = 0 \tag{3}$$

$$x = \frac{-a}{2b}$$

Thus, the optimum is defined as the Intercept Parameter Estimate divided by two times the predictor variable estimate (and, since the predictor variable is negative, this gives a positive solution). Note the plot of the actual data for SYSTEM 2, as shown in Figure 6.3. It shows the linear regression line fit to the measured data (total TCB per active initiator relative to the left Y-axis), as well as the total TCB time parabolic curve (right Y-axis). The peak of the parabolic curve indicates the highest predicted total TCB time relative to the number of active initiators. Note also that additional data points have been created from the equations for the linear regressions and the parabolic optimization equation which extend beyond the measured data (initiators 6–8 and 23–30). This better illustrates the cases of under- and over-initiation.

As expected, the corresponding graph for SYSTEM 1 indicates that fewer numbers of initiators can be supported (see Figure 6.4). This is due to

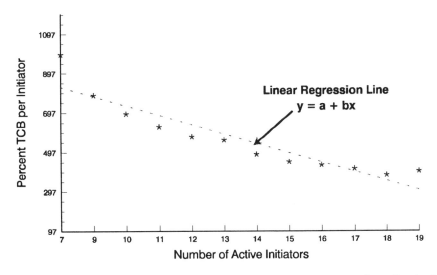

Figure 6.2 Linear regression—TCB time per initiator versus number of active initiators

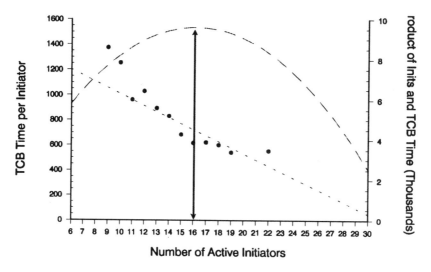

Figure 6.3 SYSTEM 2—initiator optimization

differences in storage (no ESTOR, but larger real storage) and MIPS (54 Mips available versus 75 MIPs for SYSTEM 2). In order to show the shape of the parabolic optimization curve, the data have been extended (as for SYSTEM 2) for the linear regression and parabolic equations (for initiators 1–9 and 20–27).

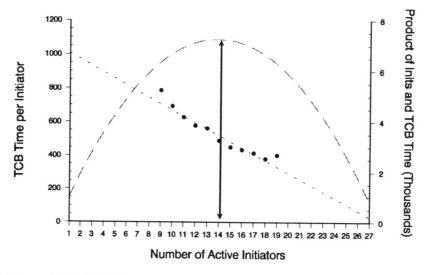

Figure 6.4 SYSTEM 1—initiator optimization

6.1.11   Determining the Optimal Number of Job Classes

The initial reason for the study was motivated by complaints of users who were experiencing delays in job startup. It was suggested by the user that another initiator should be set up to avoid the situation of "waiting too long for my jobs to start." The first area to investigate was the wait-time-to-initiate for batch jobs and the mathematics that best describe the behavior of job queuing for MVS initiators.

The job queuing and initiator characteristics for the MVS environment can be illustrated by a simple G/G/1 queuing model, which describes the average input queue wait time as a function of service time, initiator utilization, and arrival rates. Although the model is oversimplified for a complex batch processing environment typical of MVS, it does point out what can be done, theoretically, to reduce wait times. The equation that describes the average input queue wait time is:

$$\overline{w} = \frac{\sigma_{in}^2 + \sigma_{ser}^2}{\overline{ser}(1 - p)} \tag{4}$$

Where

$\overline{w}$	= the average input queue wait time
σ_{in}^2	= the variance of the interarrival time
σ_{ser}^2	= the variance of the service time
$\overline{ser}$	= the average service time
p	= the utilization of the initiator

Artis [1] points out that when the homogeneity of the distribution of the server holding times increases, i.e., lower variance, there is a reduction in the average input queue wait time. This is due to the fact that the execution time of a job is a function of the resources consumed by the job. Thus, Artis presents a strong argument in favor of resource-limited job classes as a method to reduce input queue wait time (and thus improve throughput).

A highly simplified, single job class initiator can be seen in Figure 6.5. In this model, jobs arrive and enter a queue (in this case a single job class system) where they wait until selected by the initiator. The initiator services one job at a time. When the job terminates, it exits the system.

Since the arrivals of jobs are controlled by the users, it is not a component of wait time that can be controlled by the data center. Thus, arrival rate of jobs is not an option in reducing the wait times. If we can reduce the variance of the service time, we can reduce wait time. How is this done?

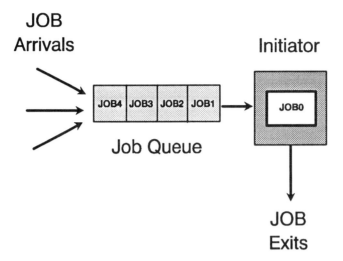

Figure 6.5 Simple initiator queuing model

According to Artis [3], the variance of the server holding time is a function of the homogeneity of the execution times of the jobs assigned to a class, and, when the homogeneity of the distribution of the server holding times increases, the variance decreases. Thus, he strongly supports the establishment and use of resource-limited job class standards.

The next stage of analysis was to determine the use of resources by job class, identify which job classes were waiting, and determine the correlation of resources to identify likely categories for cluster analysis. Cluster analysis was then used to attempt to group jobs into categories using those resources that were highly correlated. Figure 6.6 shows the average wait-time-to-initiate by job class (using the left Y-axis) and the frequency of jobs processed by each class (using the right Y-axis).

The reader should note that the largest number of jobs execute in CLASS=C (no tapes, quick jobs) and have very low wait-time-to-initiate values. On the other hand, CLASS=2 jobs (tape mounts, long-running jobs) wait a considerable time but are infrequent. This is partly due to the fact that jobs in the CLASS=2 category initiate only on the SYSTEM 1 system. In addition, CLASS=2 is only defined to one initiator.

Resource-limited job classes are based on resources such as CPU time, tape mounts, print volume, etc. A correlation analysis of resource usage to wait-time-to-initiate indicated no significant relationship. Delays experienced were due to serialization, tape drive allocation delays (after initia-

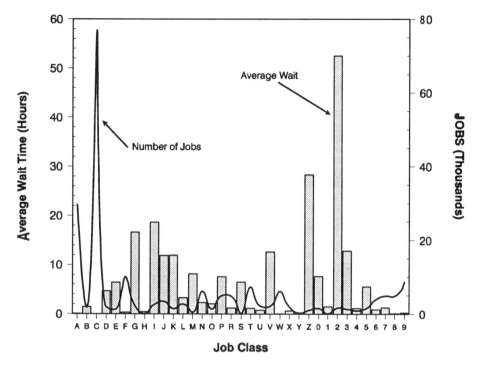

Figure 6.6 Wait-time-to-initiate and number of jobs by class—entire complex

tion), system queues, etc., rather than preinitiation resource waits. A resource correlation matrix was developed, which shows the correlation between all resource categories as well as wait time. The correlation matrix is based on all processing, over a six month period, for both domains. The strongest interresource correlation is between tape mounts and CPU time (see Table 6.3).

There is strong correlation of tape mounts to CPU time ($r = 0.728$). Due to the limitation of tape drives and MIPS, these two resources were used in a statistical cluster analysis (print lines did not provide useful discriminant criteria).

Cluster analysis is a statistical technique that helps develop job class structures by exploiting the natural patterns of resource requirements in the workload [3]. It is an iterative process in which clusters are successively approximated.

The first step in using cluster analysis is to standardize the measurements of all resource variables (CPU time, print lines and tape mounts) to a

Table 6.3 Resource Correlation Matrix

	JOBS	Average Wait	Max Wait	Average CPU	Max CPU	Average Tape	Max Tape	Avg Print	Max Print
JOBS	1								
Avg Wait	−0.189	1							
Max Wait	−0.257	0.696	1						
Avg CPU	−0.192	0.436	0.432	1					
Max CPU	−0.222	0.07	0294	0.597	1				
Avg Tape	−0.345	0.522	0.434	0.638	0.318	1			
Max Tape	−0.243	0.248	0.444	0.728	0.717	0.632	1		
Avg Prn	0.321	−0.226	−0.221	−0.312	−0.164	−0.416	−0.332	1	
Max Prn	0.837	−0.266	−0.266	−0.282	−0.202	−0.44	−0.3	0.727	1

common scale. There are two reasons for this: (1) the data points being clustered by the SAS FASTCLUS procedure perform a disjoint cluster analysis on the basis of *Euclidean distances*—thus, the metrics for distance must be within the same frame of reference (i.e., same units of measure), and (2) variables with large variances tend to have more effect on the resulting clusters than those with small variances. The SAS STANDARD procedure was used to standardize all variables to a mean of zero and variance of one. Thus, for a variable x, the standardized transform is:

$$x' = \frac{x - \bar{x}}{\sigma_x}$$

and thus

$$\sigma_x x' = x - \bar{x} \tag{5}$$

and solving for x gives

$$x = \sigma_x x' + \bar{x}$$

This last equation allows us to transform the information provided in FAST-CLUS (for example, cluster means) back into the original data values (e.g., CPU seconds, print lines, tape mounts).

A *disjoint* analysis was used to assure that the process would place each observation in one, and only one, cluster. In the *centroid* method of cluster analysis (used by FASTCLUS), the distance between two clusters is defined as the squared Euclidean distance between their means. Thus, if D_{KL} is the distance or dissimilarity measure between cluster C_K and C_L, then

$$D_{KL} = \| \bar{x}_K - \bar{x}_L \| \qquad (6)$$

Where

$\bar{x}_K$ = mean vector for cluster C_K

and

$\bar{x}_L$ = mean vector for cluster C_L.

Using a random number generator provided in the SAS language, a random sample of 10,000 jobs was chosen from the MICS database over a six month time span. Initially, five clusters were chosen using CPU time, tape mounts, and print lines. The results, as seen in Table 6.4, indicate that a very large number of jobs fall into the first cluster:

In Table 6.4, the reader should note that 9,947 jobs fell into the first cluster, and one job occurred in the third cluster (an *outlier*). The R-SQUARE values for this analysis were low for *print lines* (r^2=0.5731007) and *CPU time* (r^2=0.4568925). Thus, these two variables were eliminated in favor of *tape mounts* (r^2=0.6458169). Since only one variable, tape mounts, was significant in classifying the jobs into clusters, the use of cluster analysis was no longer necessary to categorize jobs. Earlier graphical summaries indicated that the processing environment was tape-intensive, and the resource correlation matrix also supported this conclusion.

In order to classify the tape mount jobs into their natural patterns of occurrence, several histograms were used to successively "clump" tape mounts in various frequencies. Recent data were used covering a span of 30

Table 6.4 Results of Cluster Analysis

Cluster Number	Frequency	RMS STD Deviation	Maximum Distance from Seed to Observation	Nearest Cluster	Centroid Distance
1	9947	0.6173	13.2489	5	14.5749
2	26	2.9895	10.9191	1	14.8649
3	1	0	0	5	42.5596
4	11	4.0907	14.0240	5	20.0597
5	15	4.0822	13.8010	1	14.5749

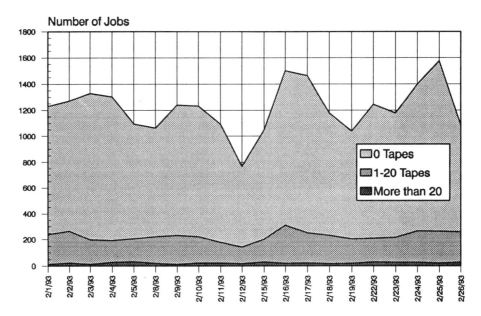

Figure 6.7 Histogram of tape usage frequency—SYSTEMS 1 & 2

days. The final result of this process was three major categories: (1) jobs that mount no (zero) tapes (this was the largest category), (2) jobs that mount 1–20 tapes, and (3) jobs that mount more than 20 tapes (very few, but very important). It is important to management that the infrequent, but critical, large tape jobs be expedited via their own job class and initiator assignments. Figure 6.7 shows how these categories are distributed over the 30-day period.

An analytic modeling system was used to support the conclusions of this study. (Note: The emphasis is on support—not prove). The modeling system, which could predict the effects on various system components of workload growth, did not estimate changes in TCB time as such. The hypothesis of overhead being in contention with application processing, as the number of initiators increased, was confirmed. In fact, the most limiting system resource (the aspect of the model that became saturated at high levels of activity) was the total system paging rate. System paging grows exponentially and exceeds acceptable levels at approximately 23 active initiators for SYSTEM 1. A series of models were run to collect paging rates at various multiprogramming levels and corresponding arrival rates. Assuming a threshold

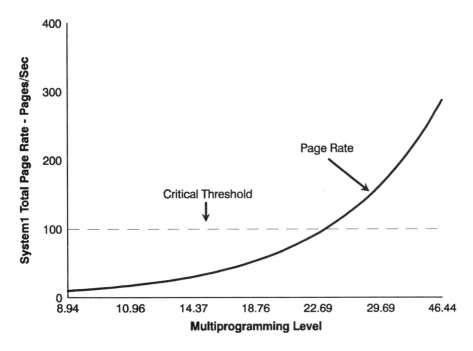

Figure 6.8 SYSTEM 1 total page rate versus multiprogramming level

of 100 pages/second as the point of unacceptable batch service (on 3380-type DASD paging devices) Figure 6.8 demonstrates potential resource exhaustion due to over-initiation.

6.2 REFERENCES

1. Artis, H. P. "How JES2 Job Classes and Initiator Structures Work." *CMG Conference Proceedings*, 1984, pp. 605–607.

2. Kuchnicki, Peter B. "Managing the Batch Workload." *EDP Performance Review* 11, no. 10 (1983): 1–6.

3. Artis, H. P. "A Technique for Establishing Resource Limited Job Class Structures." *Proceedings of the CMG Tenth International Conference on Controlled Resource Management through Computer Performance Evaluation, 1979, pp. 247–249.*

7

Capacity Planning for IBM MVS Data Storage Systems

7.1 OVERVIEW

The application of capacity planning techniques to peripheral devices and systems used in data storage is an area of intense IS focus and will continue to be important to IS planners in the years to come. As systems evolve toward networked storage, the need to plan capacity will become critical to the success of these newer, and more complex, application platforms.

IBM minframe disk systems often exceed the expense levels of any other single resource. The performance management of these systems is critical to overall systems performance. The need to balance efficient use of capacity with performance frequently results in unused capacity. This may be necessary in order to achieve performance levels required for service level objectives. As the disk environment grows, the relative proportion of disk space which is owned by operating systems and network related activites begins to diminish. At first, however, executives may feel that disk space is being "wasted" or used inefficiently.

117

7.2   DISK CAPACITY PLANNING

As with total system capacity planning, planning for disk capacity involves understanding the current capacity, the current performance levels, future systems development plans, and future corporate business plans, as well as the current level of disk technology.

7.2.1   Evaluating Current Disk Capacity

Evaluating an organization's current disk capacity means looking at more than just the total number of installed gigabytes. (One gigabyte is approximately one billion characters of information). The percentage of disk currently allocated to permanent files and the average percentage used for temporary storage are also important. To understand what happens during peak processing times, average maximum percentages also should be reviewed. This information can be gathered using various third-party utilities, or can be collected with in-house programs.

File naming conventions also play a part in evaluating the current disk capacity. Storage managers and capacity planners need to know if data is temporary or permanent, test or production, system or user. Having naming standards which categorize data by usage and ownership criteria makes measurement and forecasting possible.

In addition to naming standards, many companies use disk pooling to keep like data on a given set of disk packs. For instance, companies may have a production pool of ten disks, a test pool of five disks, and a temporary pool of ten disks. Pooling disks in this way aids in allocating and managing data on a day-to-day basis, as well as making it easier for a capacity planner to evaluate current capacity.

Another important statistic is the number and type of file accesses for each file. Files that lay dormant for a week or two, then get heavy access, then revert to dormancy, might be good candidates for data compression. Files with no accesses in 30 days probably should be archived.

Tables 7.1 and 7.2 show the type of data that might be generated when a capacity planner is evaluating current capacity on a system that uses pools to differentiate permanent from temporary storage.

Table 7.1 Sample Capacity and Percent in Use Report

Pool	Volume Serial #	Device Tracks	Allocated Tracks	Available Tracks	Available Megabytes	Percent Available
PROD	PROD01	13245	10516	2729	130	21%
	PROD02	13245	8321	4924	163	37%
	PROD03	26506	22563	3942	187	15%
	PROD04	26505	16256	10249	486	39%
TEST	TEST01	13245	11016	2229	106	17%
	TEST02	13245	6542	6703	318	51%
	TEST03	26505	20981	5524	262	21%
TEMP	TEMP01	13245	9987	3258	154	25%
	TEMP02	13245	12001	1244	59	9%

Table 7.2 Sample Data Set Name and Access Date Report

Volume Serial #	Dataset Name	Dataset Organization	Creation Date	Last Used Date	Last Modified Date	Tracks Allocated	Tracks Idle	Percent Used	Last Job Name
PROD01	PROD.LOANS.DATA	PS	10/12/92	8/13/93	8/13/93	1345	10	99%	PLOAZ
PROD01	PROD.DEPOSITS.DATA	PS	5/16/92	8/12/93	8/12/93	1569	326	79%	PDEPOSN
PROD01	PROD.HELP.DATA	PS	3/16/91	7/22/93	5/19/91	272	19	93%	NO392R
TEST01	TEST.LOANS.DATA	PS	9/9/93	9/12/93	9/14/93	134	96	28%	LOANSN
TEST02	TEST.DEPOSITS.DATA	PS	1/30/93	6/30/93	6/30/93	2798	108	96%	JKN345Y

7.2.2 Evaluating Performance

Evaluating the performance of disk storage involves looking at the minimum response times, maximum response times, and average response times for various files. When evaluating response times, it is important to know what the data represents. For instance, in most organizations, response time is generally measured as the sum of different process times such as I/O queuing (IOSQ) time, channel pending (PEND) time, seek, rotational delay, and data transfer time. These are not the response times clients complain about, because the response they see is an accumulation of the disk and CPU responses for data, plus the transmission time to a terminal, and probably some additional factors as well. When these disk response times increase,

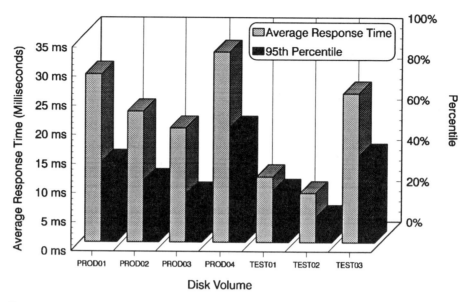

Figure 7.1 Average response times and 95th percentile rank by disk volume

however, client response times increase proportionately, so they are a major component of performance.

Increases in response time may not be a capacity problem. Problems like channel contention also may cause performance degradation, as will file fragmentation and bad blocking. These things make it appear that more disk is needed, when what is really required is I/O tuning of the files or file distributions. Disk I/O factors may create enormous performance impacts. Disk access is typically the slowest link in the chain of events which comprise response time and can contribute as much as 70% of the total.

Most organizations working with service-level agreements have response time and other reporting systems already in place. If not, there are utilities available for extracting and analyzing performance data.

Figures 7.1 and 7.2 show the type of data that might be generated when a capacity planner is evaluating current performance.

7.2.3 Estimating Future Requirements

Estimating future disk storage requirements starts with a review of present and historical use. This review might include a formal regression analysis on the historical data, as shown in Figure 7.3, where a capacity planner has

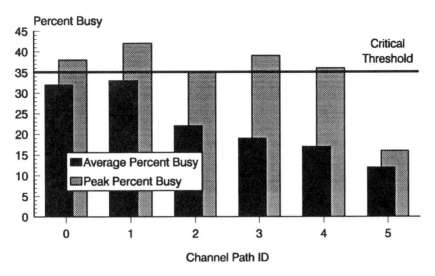

Figure 7.2 Disk channel path activity—average and average peak percent busy

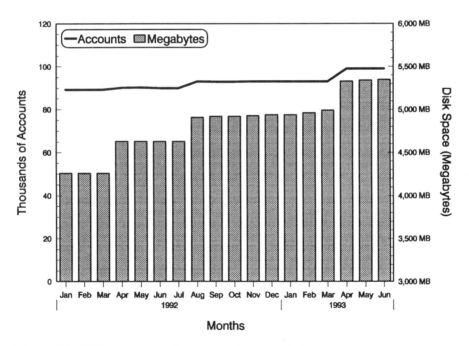

Figure 7.3 Disk space growth compared to growth in accounts

tracked the growth of disk versus the number of accounts at a bank. In smaller organizations, the analysis may be just a review based on previous experience. As a rule of thumb, capacity planners estimate 15 percent to 30 percent growth per year, then add or subtract other requirements such as acquiring new corporations, or downsizing to midrange systems.

Figure 7.4 shows the resulting capacity forecast of the data in Figure 7.3. The small step increases in disk usage represent the acquisitions of other businesses, while the lower sloped intervals between show normal growth. To anticipate the effect of a larger acquisition, a regression analysis was done on the historical data, then the growth equation was calculated and predicted account increases were derived. The corresponding jump in disk capacity is shown in the "Forecast Requirements" section of the chart.

While a formal procedure may seem like a lot of work, it can be kept up to date with relative ease, and it is generally more objective than an "educated" guess. Some IS organizations have actually included a formal report in their Request For Proposals (RFP) for new equipment. This lets them say, "This is our history, these are our requirements, what do you have that will meet

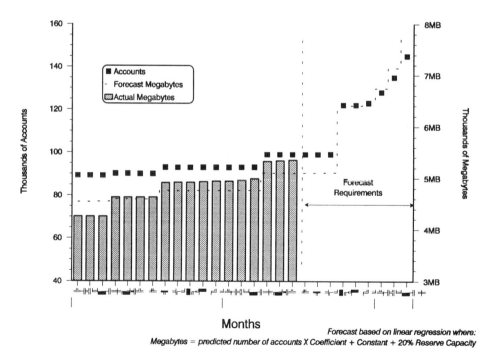

Forecast based on linear regression where:
Megabytes = predicted number of accounts X Coefficient + Constant + 20% Reserve Capacity

Figure 7.4 Linear regression forecast of megabytes using accounts as predictor

them?" Vendors can address specific issues, and the IS organization has an objective measurement tool.

For estimates to be valuable, even when using a formal estimating system, there must be some control over data set allocation. If users allocate data wherever and whenever they like, data sets can mushroom. At a minimum, this lack of control increases CPU cycles and I/O counts as the storage manager runs jobs to move data in order to balance I/O activity for optimal performance. Ultimately, users suffer poor system performance and I/O response degrades.

To make the best use of current and future disk capacity, the data should be well blocked. Blocking places data records together, with no gaps between them, only between the blocks. Most blocking schemes work with full-track or half-track blocking, and depend on the specific type of disk (disk geometry). Calculating an appropriate block-size can be tedious. Many IS organizations have written or purchased a utility to do the arithmetic. Due to the relationship of the access methods in the operating system and the storage device geometry, 'full track' blocking techniques greatly improve I/O performance as well as reduce "wasted" space.

Calculating the disk space a data set requires is also important. Since cylinder and track use depend on the block size of the file and type of disk on which it resides, the numbers can vary considerably. A 120 cylinder file on a 3380 may or may not be larger than a 110 cylinder file on a 3390. Working in megabytes (millions of characters) allows the capacity planner to compare data set sizes and more accurately predict increases. As with block size, the number of megabytes is also generally calculated by a program.

There are also operating environment issues to consider when estimating future requirements. For instance, the size of drives and the space available in the computer room could limit the number of new drives. The new drives (3390s and compatibles) have smaller "footprints," giving more capacity per square foot of room, but if insufficient floor space is available for the 3390s, size is definitely a concern.

One way around the size constraints might be to use channel-extending technology to move peripherals out of the data center altogether.

7.2.4 Evaluating Alternatives

When capacity planners consider going to higher-density 3390 disks, the higher density can actually be wasted when a data set needs single access data to meet response time requirements. Some MVS/ESA features, such as

LSR pools, speed I/O without a storage manager placing a data set on a high-speed volume. Before capacity planners decide that new disk capacity is needed to meet response time requirements, they should check with their systems programmers to explore these operating system features.

Another alternative for lowering response times without increasing disk capacity is caching. Caching works as a high speed, solid state intermediary between a storage device, generally disk or cartridge tape, and a system requesting data. When a read request is sent to the disk, the cache intercepts it. It checks to see if it has already accessed this data, and if it has, it sends it back to the system. No request is passed on to the much slower rotational disk, significantly speeding response time. When the data is not already in cache, it is read from disk, but subsequent requests can be processed directly through the cache. This is especially beneficial to applications doing sequential read processing.

By using caching, an IS organization can see up to an 80% improvement in on-line inquiry response times. It also can speed up backups to tape, thereby increasing the batch window.

While caching can be used when updating data, it is generally not a good idea. It can actually degrade response times because the cached data must be updated in two places: on the actual storage device, and in cache. There are various storage techniques that can minimize the degradation, such as only updating the cache, but these can lead to integrity problems in a system crash. Write caching utilizes techniques to "destage" the disk I/O asychronously with MVS I/O operations. Nevertheless, for applications requiring inquiry only, caching can have a real value.

7.2.5 Changing Hardware

If the capacity plan calls for a change in hardware, the change can range from adding an additional device of the same model to upgrading all disks to the latest (currently 3390) technology. Adding another same-model disk is relatively painless and quite common. Upgrading to new technology can be a tedious process.

Implementing 3390 technology is a four-step process. First, the storage manager must verify that all the software that will be using the new drives supports the 3390s. If not, new software releases must be ordered and installed before any hardware changes can be made.

Next, the data being migrated must be analyzed. Some organizations simply move data sets, but this does not take advantage of the new capacity of the 3390s. While this approach may be okay for VSAM data sets, partitioned data sets and sequential data sets should be reblocked for efficiency. Once data is blocked to maximize the new 3390 track sizes, it cannot be moved back to 3380s without reblocking. Most organizations do not need to go back anyway; going back to 3380 technology is time-consuming.

Next, programs and JCL should be examined. To make use of the new blocking factors, some old programs and JCL may require changes.

The last step involves the actual movement of the data. This can be done either all at once, or as a data set goes through its normal reorganization process. The method used will depend on how frequently data sets must be deleted and reorganized. If most data sets go through this process at least once a week, reorganization would be the best method, as long as all new allocations are redirected to the new devices.

7.2.6 Trend to System-Managed Storage (SMS)

Any discussion of disk capacity planning would be incomplete without exploring the trend to System-Managed Storage (SMS), a disk management concept based on SHARE and GUIDE user recommendations of the late 1970s and early 1980s. IBM's implementation of SMS is a series of software products first released in the late 1980s. Specifics of the IBM software will be discussed later, but the general idea of SMS is to feed desired system parameters such as maximum response time into the system and, based on parameters, data set names, and other criteria, have the system select appropriate, non-volume-specific disks to hold the data.

The four categories of parameters are Data Class, Management Class, Storage Class, and Storage Group. In the Data Class parameters, the storage administrator sets up the physical data set characteristics such as record length, space, data set organization, and block size. These record characteristics are passed on to a data set at allocation time based on the low-level qualifier in the data set name. For example, a JCL data set might have a record length of 80 and an organization of physical sequential, whereas a LOAD data set might be a partitioned data set with a block size of 32760. Any data set named xxxxxx.xxxx.JCL would inherit the JCL data set characteristics.

Management Class parameters specify how frequently a data set should be backed up, how many backups to save, how long a data set should be dormant before it is archived, and how over-allocated space should be released.

With Storage Class parameters, a storage administrator can specify data set service levels in terms of millisecond response times. Storage Groups, on the other hand, are specific disks with similar performance thresholds that are available for different kinds of data sets. The concept of Storage Groups should be familiar to most administrators already working with disk pools.

There are several benefits to SMS. To applications programmers, for instance, SMS can take the drudgery out of JCL. In many shops, decisions on block sizes, how much space to use, and what disk to put data on are often the responsibility of programmers. Instead, simple SMS JCL statements can be used, increasing application programmers productivity by unburdening them of this error prone task. Third-party packages that create job flows from JCL code can recognize the new SMS JCL commands, making job flow creation easier as well.

In addition to relieving the programmers, SMS helps reduce the number of incorrectly allocated data sets that a storage manager would have to correct. The storage manager sets up data set parameters that SMS follows, so SMS can actually enforce new naming and allocation standards. By decreasing the amount of time a storage manager spends moving data around, SMS can save a company about 20% of the storage manager's time.

SMS can also reduce wasted disk space. Once data set retention information is set up in the Management Class parameters, SMS can identify and archive old data. Not only does this clear data off disk faster, but the storage manager doesn't have to move the data manually, saving even more administration time.

Perhaps the greatest benefit of SMS, however, is the ease in upgrading to new disks. Because the system takes care of allocations, migrations, file-size changes and the like, data sets have device independence. A data set can be recreated at the optimum efficiency on the new drives, saving hundreds of hours of conversion time.

As SMS is implemented today, there are also some drawbacks because nothing is perfect. Before a complete IBM SMS solution can be used, an organization must be at or above the following software levels:

MVS/ESA
MVS/DFP 3.1
DFHSM 2.4

DFDSS 2.4
DFSORT 10
RACF 1.8

Some experts are also recommending these products at or above these levels:

RMF 4.1
TSO/E 1.4 or 2.1
ISPF/PDF 2.3

Since many organizations are back one or more releases, they have to do all the conversions involved to upgrade to the required level. While some third party software packages can be substituted for IBM products, most organizations still need to upgrade to the current version of the third-party products.

Because data set characteristics are based on the low-level qualifier in a data set name, an IS organization must also convert all data set names to follow the new SMS naming conventions. Even if organizations have strictly enforced data set naming conventions, this requires a great deal of work in actual renaming and in JCL changes. It might take months for large organizations to do this.

After all the conversions, the technology is not quite ready for full use. Uncatalogued data sets, VSAM catalogued data sets, and data sets referenced in JOBCATS or STEPCATS cannot be placed under SMS control. While some of these restrictions are being addressed, ISAM and system pack allocations may never be SMS-controllable. With all this effort, an organization can realistically expect to automate only about 60% of its disk.

An organization also must invest in more disk capacity for the conversion effort. SMS and non-SMS data cannot reside on the same packs, so at least one new disk must be brought in for a conversion volume.

The last drawback of SMS is that it's hard to determine if the performance parameters set up in the management class are actually met. SMS tries to allocate a data set on a volume that meets both performance and space criteria, but if it can not, it still allocates on a pack to meet the space criteria. Additional diagnostic software is needed to check on the actual performance levels.

Still, most organizations can realize performance increases and more efficient use of current resources from using an SMS system.

7.2.7   Software Available

Even without going to a full implementation of SMS, there are several tools available to help storage managers and capacity planners in analyzing the current environment. One of these is DMS/OS from Sterling Software. With DMS/OS, a storage manager or capacity planner can perform exception analyses, check on the active files, and automatically archive those that are inactive. Innovation Data Processing's product groups FDR/ABR/CPK perform similar functions, as does CA-ASM2 from Computer Associates.

Performance tuning products include DASDMON from Dusquene Systems and CA-FASTDASD from Computer Associates.

If an organization decides to implement SMS, it can do so in a variety of ways. Some may choose all products from one vendor while others may decide to mix-and-match the products. The three main vendors of SMS software, and some specifics about their product lines appear below.

In the late 1980s IBM introduced its DFSMS line of products. The five products are MVS/DFP, DFHSM, DFDSS, DFSORT, and RACF. MVS/DFP takes care of about half of the SMS capabilities, including allocation and device support. DFHSM handles the data backup and recovery functions and controls migrating inactive data sets to other storage media. DFDSS is a companion of DFHSM, performing the actual data set moves. The last two products, DFSORT and RACF perform the functions they are traditionally associated with, sorting and securing data. In SMS, RACF has the additional job of securing the SMS control programs and functions.

Another line of SMS products is SAMS from Sterling software. Also an integration of existing products, SAMS consists of VAM, DMS, and SHRINK, plus a new Automatic Initiation Manager (AIM) and a PC-based monitoring system called VIEW. Most of the SAMS features work similar to those of DFSMS, but SAMS has some additional capabilities. For example, it can manage some types of data that DFSMS cannot and it allows 3380s and 3390s to be in the same storage group.

A third SMS alternative is the Computer Associates ASM line of products, consisting of CA-ASM2 and other products such as CA-FASTDASD, CA-IENF, CA-SORT, and CA-ACF2. An interesting note about the CA offerings is that they run across multiple platforms, including some products for both VSE and VM.

As mentioned earlier, some of these products can be mixed and matched. For instance, CA-SORT and CA-ACF2 could replace DFSORT and RACF, or SYNCSORT could replace CA-SORT.

Disk capacity planning is a complicated process, so these are just some of the things to consider when developing a plan. Disk is not the only storage medium planners have available; however, they need to consider tape and perhaps some new, evolving technologies that will be discussed later.

7.3   TAPE AND TAPE DRIVE CAPACITY PLANNING

Planning for tape and tape drive capacity also involves understanding the current capacity, future systems development plans, and future corporate business plans, as well as the current level of tape technology. Because tapes are used primarily for disk backup in many organizations, tape capacity requirements also depend on future disk requirement.

7.3.1   Tape Processing—Evaluating Current Capacity

Just as disk capacity is more than how many gigabytes of storage are available, tape capacity is more than how many tapes and drives a company has, and how many gigabytes they'll hold. Because tape media is stored separately from the tape drives, the storage capacity is essentially unlimited except for the physical constraints of space and the limits of keeping track of the tape volumes. In addition, the use of tape operators may be a factor in the case of tape systems which are only partially automated. Tape *drive* capacity, is of particular concern to systems operations since a lack of drives can dramatically lower throughput (and, for IBM MVS systems, results in workload interruptions due to tape drive allocation delays). Let us first examine the problem of tape drive capacity, then the problem of tape (medial) capacity.

From the perspective of tape drive *capacity management*, an analysis of tape drive allocations on an hourly basis should be performed. Expressed as a percentage of tape drive capacity, the percent of capacity allocated per hour gives some idea of the usage pattern of the drives over the 24 hour work day. This will typically include peaks and valleys which, in turn, help identify opportunities to move more tape processing to less busy time periods. Unfortunately, many batch workloads are not movable without missing important deadlines. For an example of tape drive usage patterns see Figure 7.5.

Frequently, the need for additional tape drive capacity results from the requirement of meeting the demands for *concurrent* tape mounts during a peak interval of time. In Figure 7.5, for example, the combined maximum hourly tape drive usage for several mainframe systems reaches a peak on

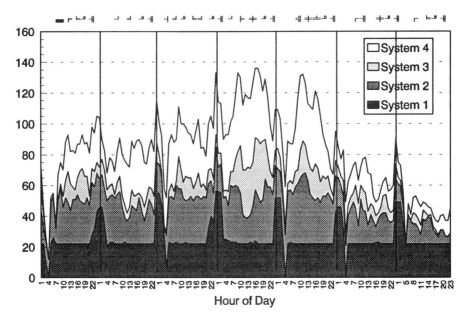

Figure 7.5 Tape drive usage patterns in a tape intensive environment

Thursday during the afternoon hours. If the workload cannot be rescheduled (unmovable for whatever reasons), and jobs are waiting extremely long (too long to meet promised batch deadline requirements), then additional drives may be required even if they then remain idle during most of the other days of the week. Strategic reserves to meet the unexpected (and usually unforecasted) surge in tape usage can be evaluated from a risk benefit basis. What are the risks to revenue of delayed tape processing? What are the benefits of quicker service? Are the costs worth the benefits?

There are short term benefits to changing the workloads themselves in order to effectively manage tape processing. Many tape mounts are due to applications which backup versions of datasets during production processing in order to assist in restarting long batch jobs.

It's not uncommon for organizations to have more than 100,000 tapes, but at any point in time, many of them may be completely blank, or holding only one-tenth their capacity. Then the capacity planner must analyze current capacity by considering total tapes plus these numbers: the percentage of the total that are blank, the percentage of the total that are scratch, the number of generations required for each backup tape, the retention period of each tape, and the number of tapes in off-site storage.

What percentage of the total is blank is important because blank tapes usually occur when a file is no longer being used, but is still backed up. Whatever the reason for the blank tapes, valuable resources are being wasted in creating and storing them, leaving them unavailable for valid data.

At first glance, the percent scratch may seem the same as the percentage blank, but scratch tapes are tapes that usually have been written on, but it's old data now, so the tapes are slated to be rewritten again. Scratch tapes need to be available for processing each night, and if there aren't enough of them, backups and other processing can't run.

In order to adequately predict any future increase or decrease in tape backups, the capacity planner also needs to look at the average number of generations per data set. While tapes are usually used for backup, which relates them to the amount of disk, critical data sets may need ten or more generations simultaneously available. This increases the disk to tape ratio.

The last concern for the capacity planner is the average retention period for each tape. Some backups and archived tapes must be kept for seven years or more and many are duplicated for off-site disaster recovery storage. Like generation data sets, if a large portion of the tapes on hand must be stored for some length of time, the actual number of usable tapes can be greatly decreased.

7.3.2 Estimating Future Requirements

Once the capacity planner understands the current tape environment, planning for the number of tapes is fairly straightforward. The planner can estimate requirements by taking the forecasted increase in disk use and multiplying all current tape capacity categories by a scaling factor based on the correlation of tape usage to disk capacity. With this new number, the planner can add or subtract requirements for percent blank, percent scratch, number of generations and predicted retention periods, based on the business plan. For instance, a change in accounting procedures, or in government reporting regulations, might increase or decrease the number of tapes on long-term retention. Mergers and acquisitions can also increase the number of tapes needed.

Systems development applications can increase the need for tapes, just as they can increase the need for disk. A new system can take hundreds of tapes when it is first turned over to production because all generations are set up ahead of time. They may be blank for months, but they need to be there.

Also, the old tapes should be archived in case the new application ever needs to be backed out.

The capacity planner must also consider the tape requirements of the capacity plan itself requires. Storing the historical SMF data for eighteen months may take hundreds of tapes.

After a new capacity number is determined, the capacity planner should double-check with the disaster recovery people to see if any additional capacity is needed for off-site storage.

Just as there are physical limits for the number of disk drives that can fit into a data center, the size of tape drives also can cause limitations. This is not usually a big problem for data centers as the availability for tape storage room. Some data centers have over one hundred thousand tapes, taking up considerably more room than tape drives.

If the capacity plan calls for a large increase in the number of tapes, storage could be a problem. One way around the physical limitations is to use channel extenders, as mentioned in the disk section.

7.3.3 Evaluating Alternatives

Until recently, the only choices involved with tape were the number of bits per inch (bpi) to store data and what length reel to use. In the last few years, a new type of tape has appeared on the tape cartridges scene. As the Table 7.1 capacity chart shows, cartridges hold more than traditional reels, yet they are much smaller (about the size of a Beta VCR cartridge) and easier to store. Cartridges are also sturdier than reels and have lower data error rates.

For these reasons, most data centers have or are migrating to cartridge format. When converting to cartridges, there are some compatibility issues to consider. While cartridges are more efficient, IS organizations that need to transfer tapes to non-IBM sites, or to IBM sites that have not yet converted to cartridge, need to keep at least one reel tape drive and some reel tapes. In the long-term non-IBM sites will probably adopt cartridge technology, but for now, reels are still a necessity.

Another reason to keep a reel tape drive might be to read archived data, since it is not generally converted.

Changing to new tape technology is relatively painless. Many sites start using the new drives for their current backups, and the reels disappear by attrition. If there is a large volume of archived data that is critical, some data centers also convert this data.

7.3.4 Software Available

Because tapes are used to back up data, it's important that the correct backups be available in the event of a disk failure or other means of data corruption. A tape that is accidentally scratched can make recovery nearly impossible. To minimize this possibility, many IS organizations use software to manage the scratching and retaining of tapes. The most popular system available today is Computer Associates' CA-1. Originally named Tape Management System (TMS), the product was written in 1971.

CA-1 allows a storage manager to define life cycles for each tape, and when the specified number of cycles has passed, CA-1 automatically scratches the tape.

A nice feature of CA-1 is that cycles can be set up by absolute numbers or by specific dates. If a tape cycle is set up for a number such as ten, and the tape is created daily, after the tenth day the first tape will be scratched. If the tape is created annually, however, the first tape will be held for ten years. With the date method of setting up a cycle, the storage manager would say scratch this tape on a specific date, or in five days from creation, or some other date-specific reference. When that date passes, then the tape is scratched.

Since tape technology has been relatively stable for the past decade or so, tape capacity planning is a fairly straightforward process. Still, a capacity planner who is aware of all the available storage media choices will be better able to meet future business needs at the minimum cost. Some technologies to keep an eye on are described next.

7.4 EVOLVING TECHNOLOGIES

In addition to the traditional disk and tape storage methods, today's capacity planner might be able to increase capacity using new techniques on the current media, such as data compression, or new storage devices such as optical disk and RAID (redundant arrays of inexpensive disks), or new access

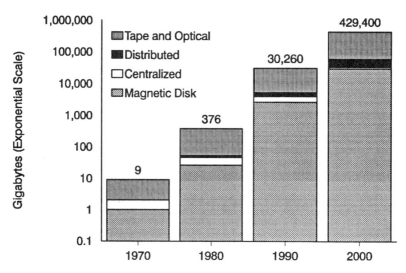

Figure 7.6 The exponential growth of electronic data in a typical Fortune 500 corporation (in gagabytes)

devices such as automated tape libraries. Just as with SMS, use of each of these is increasing, and each has its own benefits and drawbacks.

7.5   DATA COMPRESSION

To save disk and tape space, many organizations are turning to data compression. This usually means running data through a program that takes out irrelevant information, such as spaces, thereby squeezing a lot more relevant data in smaller areas. Depending on the data being compressed, organizations can see an 80 percent reduction in space requirements, especially in their tape backups.

There are drawbacks to data compression, however. Compression can actually degrade response time when used for certain disk-based applications. Because another layer of software is involved in storing and retrieving the data, the machine wastes valuable cycles. To be worthwhile, data compression on disk should be static. Text files for on-line help systems would be good candidates for compression, because they are not accessed frequently, but must be on-line.

To determine which data to compress on disk, the storage manager should review the pattern of access for the various files, looking for low access, and low volume data that still requires quick response times when it is accessed. This will yield a good candidate list.

Data compression to tape should almost be a given today. The type of data that resides on tape usually requires little access, and response time isn't an issue. By compressing the data, IS organizations can reduce tape usage by nearly 50%. The only time to reconsider compressing data on tape is when small additional delays compound to close the batch window. For many organizations, a wider batch window is more important than the number of tapes that can be saved by compression. This is another reason the capacity planner must consider all the aspects of an IS department's service when making out a capacity plan.

Two data compression products a storage manager might consider are SHRINK from Sterling Software, available in MVS, IMS, and DB2 versions, and Innovation Access Method (IAM) from Innovation Data Processing. SHRINK can choose compression levels to minimize system degrading yet still give some storage relief. IAM is especially good at VSAM file compressing, providing a 50 to 70 percent reduction.

7.6 OPTICAL DISKS

Optical disks, unlike traditional disks, are nonmagnetic. Instead of magnetizing a surface to store data, optical disks use a laser to etch in the information. Optical disks can be used to store complete images and full motion video, as some imaging systems and interactive videodiscs do, or they can be used to store vast amounts of digital data. When used to store images, they generally replace file cabinets, but when used to store digital data, they can replace tape and disk storage.

Optical disks come in two main sizes: 12" and 5". The 5" disks are generally used in PCs with CD-ROM players, but the 12" disk is generally used for image processing systems or optical storage for mainframes. The benefits for the mainframe user are staggering. One 12" optical disk can store 2GB of information, whereas an entire 3380-K can store only 1.9GB.

The CD-ROM players that are used on PCs typically hold single disks, but the 12" disks are often found in optical disk "jukeboxes." Similar to a record jukebox, they take the requests for data from the host system, retrieve the

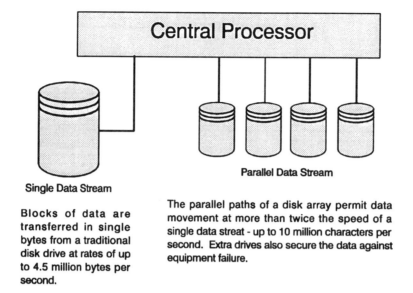

Central Processor

Parallel Data Stream

Single Data Stream

Blocks of data are transferred in single bytes from a traditional disk drive at rates of up to 4.5 million bytes per second.

The parallel paths of a disk array permit data movement at more than twice the speed of a single data streat - up to 10 million characters per second. Extra drives also secure the data against equipment failure.

Figure 7.7 How disk arrays work

correct optical disk from inside the jukebox storage area, and load it into the drive for processing.

While optical disk technology has been around for more than a decade, and it can significantly reduce the need for disk and tape, few IS departments have installed optical disk storage systems. There are two main reasons for this lack of acceptance. The disks in most optical systems can be written to only once and they are relatively slow for data retrieval.

Allowing data to be written only once makes the data permanent, while most IS data is interactive and very dynamic. For this reason, organizations using optical disks today generally use it as a replacement for tapes that contain archive information.

The slowness of disks is a real concern in today's on-line world. Often compounding disks' speed problem is the fact that they need to emulate a traditional storage device to work correctly. Adding a layer of emulation software makes response times even slower by adding additional work to the CPU.

Until the write-once and slowness issues can be addressed, most optical disks will probably be used in image processing systems or for archive purposes.

7.7   AUTOMATED TAPE LIBRARIES

With the advent of the new tape cartridges came a way to access data stored on tape without human intervention. Automated tape libraries store hundreds (even thousands) of the new tape cartridges and then load them as requested, much the same way optical disk systems store and retrieve their disks.

In addition to faster access to any given tape, automated tape libraries eliminate the need for operator tape mounts, and they are in a self-contained storage unit. When purchasing an automated tape library, a storage manager knows from the start there is room for a specific number of tapes. This also eases the capacity planner's job.

The main drawback to automated tape libraries is their cost, running from around $200,000 to more than a million. Just eliminating an operator or two, or decreasing the amount of tape storage space, could not justify costs. If data stored on tape needs to be accessed quickly, however, an organization can justify the expense versus equivalent disk storage capacity.

7.8   REDUNDANT ARRAYS OF INDEPENDENT DISKS (RAID)

Instead of using the single large expensive disks (SLED) found in traditional disk storage systems, RAID technology uses arrays of 5" or 3" disks. This approach gives an equal or better performance than traditional systems because small requests can be handled separately, while large requests are filled in parallel.

Touted as a less expensive, more reliable alternative to traditional disk storage, RAID technology has yet to prove it can deliver. One concern of many IS people is that with more disks comes the possibility of more downtime. As applications continue to go on-line, IS organizations can't risk downtime. RAID vendors have responded to this increased risk by including disk mirroring or parity checking in their systems. While these methods increase the reliability of RAID systems, they also increase the cost. Some analysts say RAID technology may actually be more expensive than traditional storage for the next five to ten years.

Even with drawbacks, vendor development of RAID devices is expanding. Some forms of array technology are available now such as the dual copy function on IBM 3990 class control units and EMC's Symmetrix ICDA, or will shortly be available such as StorageTek's recently announced ICEBERG. Because RAID is still evolving, only a few capacity planners are currently looking at it. As the technology continues to grow, it will become an important consideration for all capacity planners.

7.9 CONCLUSION

Information Systems departments cannot afford to underestimate the capacity of their systems. The future of the department and the company depends on reliable, efficient systems. By using capacity planning, an IS department can minimize future storage problems.

Planners should keep abreast of 3390 and other new drives for disk storage. They need to investigate System Managed Storage because this trend will continue, although its maximum benefits are still limited.

Data compression will also become more important in the future. Organizations can identify data best suited to compression, and capacity planners can reduce their hardware requirements without increasing response times.

Tape capacity planning is in fairly good control. With software to control the generations, retention periods, and scratching of tape reels and tape cartridges, current use is easy to determine, and future needs are predictable. Still, the number of organizations implementing automated tape libraries will continue to increase.

As the speed of optical disk storage systems improves, and as RAID proves it can deliver, the traditional storage methods will be partially replaced, giving capacity planners more options for meeting the business needs of their companies.

8

Charting and Graphics Presentations for Capacity Planning

8.1 OVERVIEW

One of the important steps in every capacity analysis study is the presentation of the results of data analyses in such a manner that critical decision support information can be understood and evaluated by decision makers. Busy managers like clear and expressive graphic summaries that clearly illustrate the important information that should be examined, evaluated, and acted upon. Frequently, the reader of capacity planning reports is not an expert in descriptive statistics, forecasting metrics, or even computer metrics. It is also usually the case that the recommendations of capacity planners are very expensive. It is therefore especially critical for the capacity planner's reports, in a business context, to be clear, as jargon-free as possible, and require minimum effort from the reader.

Why use charts? Is it because "a picture is worth a thousand words"? Not exactly. If this were true, then I could ask someone to draw me a picture of the Declaration of Independence! Since the invention of analytic geometry and statistical graphics, we might say that a picture is worth a thousand numbers. Measurement-intensive disciplines, such as capacity planning and performance management, are also number intensive. Thanks to computing, the sheer bulk of "tabular data" can be overwhelming.

Pickover [1], an authority on application mathematics and computer graphics, identifies the important applications of computer graphics in the following areas: (1) revealing hidden correlations and unexpected relationships (and as an adjunct numerical analysis), (2) simulating nature, and (3) providing a source of general scientific intuition. It is the first category, plus the need to communicate the information, that is the focal point of this chapter.

Computer graphics serves two primary purposes within the context of capacity planning:

1. Revealing patterns and relationships in the data (for the analyst)

2. Communicating the information expressed by these relationships and patterns rather than merely presenting the data (for the decision maker or manager)

The efforts of technical analysts to develop graphical materials to summarize data, as well as the rise of graphical user interface (GUI) use in the desktop technology areas, suggest that the characterization and detection of significant information in data, or procedures that manipulate data, are fundamentally visual. Excellent guidelines for the presentation of data that are appropriate within the context of capacity planning have been written by Jain [2], Finehirsh [3], MacKinnon [4], Powell [5], Schmid [6], and Tufte [7].

Earlier works on this subject stressed broad guidelines. For example, Schmid associates good graphics with the following characteristics: accuracy, simplicity, clarity, neat appearance, and logically structured. More recent works, for example by Jain, attribute goodness in graphics with the following, more detailed, guidelines:

1. Require minimum effort from the reader.

2. Maximize information: There should be sufficient information on the graph to make it self-sufficient.

3. Minimize ink: Present as much information as possible with as little ink as possible.

4. Use commonly accepted practices: Present what people expect.

5. Avoid ambiguity.

In addition, Jain (who is very good at pointing out common mistakes) identifies a number of practices that he advises the reader to avoid:

1. Presenting too many alternatives on a single chart
2. Presenting many y-variables on a single chart
3. Using symbols in place of text
4. Placing extraneous information on the chart
5. Selecting scale ranges improperly
6. Using a line chart in place of a column chart

8.2 GENERAL SUGGESTIONS FOR SUCCESSFUL DATA PRESENTATION

Learn how to use PC-based graphics software. Large systems graphics software tends to be extremely difficult to use, costly to run, and hard to maintain. Generally, the desktop technology platforms provide superior quality and ease of use as well as the ability to link the data of analysis activity (spreadsheets) to graphics—to a figure in the final document (Object Linking and Embedding). Most business-oriented graphics software will do the job. Scientific graphics packages can do more but can also be more complex. Perhaps the advantage of scientific graphics software is that it often includes the capability for automating many curve-fitting routines.

For reports that are lengthy or will be photocopied, use black and white charts, rather than color. This is also less expensive. For presentations, color can be used effectively—for example, with slides or overhead transparencies. Be aware that the colors you see on the screen may not be exactly the same on paper (this often requires some experimenting).

Skill with graphical presentations tends to be an art. You will develop skill and style the more you do it. Expect your first graphics to be rather disappointing. If possible, get some training or work with someone who has experience with graphics. Experiment.

Powell suggests that unless the shape of the data suggests otherwise, the horizontal or x-axis should be the longer axis. Tufte attributes this to the following: There is a physical analogy to scanning the horizon, an easier task than vertical scanning; it is easier to avoid the use of vertical labeling; and it tends to emphasize causal influences, because the x-axis is usually associated with the "cause" variable and the y-axis with the "effect" variable.

Finehirsh recommends the use of successive levels of detail when presenting graphics data. For example, if you are showing the average daily CPU utilization for several days, subsequent charts would show average hourly CPU utilization for the same period. Or, perhaps additional charts would show only charts that explore the details of exception thresholds identified in earlier charts. Finehirsh has developed a Windows product that allows the dynamic display of numerous system measurements and enables "drill-down" features to explore exception conditions. In addition, trends can be quickly generated (see iMETRICS in the appendix). This shows promise for using graphics to quickly assess the health of a system. As graphics becomes easier to use and less costly, the problem for management becomes the same as it was for tabular data—too many graphs. Using successive levels of detail, either in printed reports or interactively on a PC, can help alleviate the problem of "information overload."

8.2.1 Labeling the Chart, Data, and Axes

The title of the chart should be clear and concise. Since most capacity planning charts are plotting data over time, the title should explicitly identify the time interval. For example, "CPU Seconds Utilized" is rather uncertain (unless one notices the x-axis) compared to "CPU Seconds Utilized per Day." If the data values are calculated rather than measured—for example, a plot of "average" daily CPU seconds used with an explanation concerning the calculation in the curve label, legend, or title, such as "Average CPU Seconds Utilized per Day."

Most experts agree that direct, in-plot, text annotation (see Figure 8.1) is preferable to the use of a legend (see Figure 8.2). This is primarily the case with a line graph consisting of only three or four lines. This is also best used for a one-time graph. If the data relationships, and thus the lines, are likely to change as new data are reported, it becomes very tedious to reposition the annotations. Where graphs change frequently, as in a monthly report, legends are easier to implement with most graphics packages.

When legends are used, it is best to be as explicit as possible. Make sure the lines are sufficiently different by using dashed lines, dots, different shades, and/or different line widths. In my own experience, using more

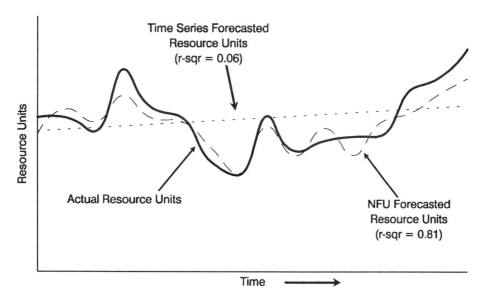

Figure 8.1 Line chart with annotation makes identification of data easy

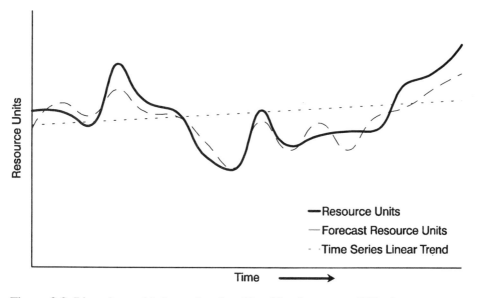

Figure 8.2 Line chart with legend makes identification more difficult

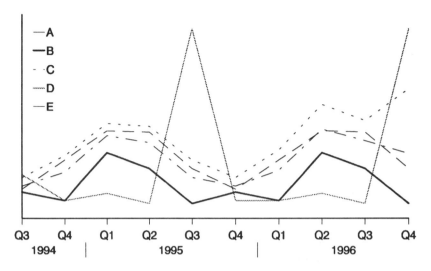

Figure 8.3 Multiple lines in a chart may be confusing

than four lines gets too confusing, and it is difficult to distinguish between lines (see Figure 8.3). In this situation, a combination of lines and bars (and maybe dots) may be best (see Figure 8.4).

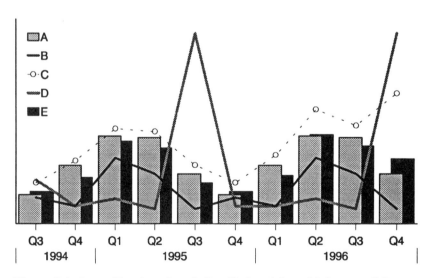

Figure 8.4 A combination chart helps distinguish multiple sets of data

8.3   BAR CHARTS

Bar charts, if only one variable is being charted, can do without a legend or a label if the title describes the variable being displayed. If the bar represents, for example, system *availability* (a common service-level metric), then both labeling and the amount of ink (relative to the amount of information) influence the criteria for presentation. Bar charts are a good choice for displaying a single variable when the number of bars is about 30 or less.

Most computer system environments report system or service availability as a vertical bar chart (see Figure 8.5). The problem with this chart is that it uses a lot of ink in proportion to the amount of information (the bars change very little). A much better chart would be to chart the *unavailability* of the system (see Figure 8.6). Even this may be a problem in a service-level administration context because the actual numbers, as well as the history (to see if things are getting better or worse), may need to be reported (it is irritating to try to guess the values from a chart). In this case, the solution may be a data table (see Figure 8.7) or use of data labels above each bar (see Figure 8.8). The bottom line: Show a chart with a data table when details are necessary.

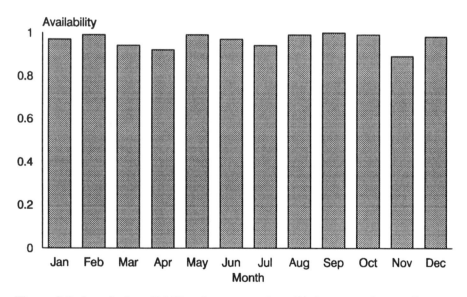

Figure 8.5 A typical availability chart uses a lot of ink to reveal a small amount of information

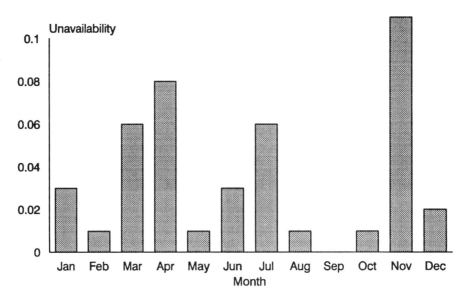

Figure 8.6 A chart of the same data defined as unavailability provides more information with less ink

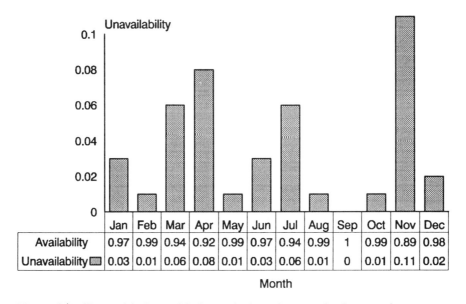

	Jan	Feb	Mar	Apr	May	Jun	Jul	Aug	Sep	Oct	Nov	Dec
Availability	0.97	0.99	0.94	0.92	0.99	0.97	0.94	0.99	1	0.99	0.89	0.98
Unavailability	0.03	0.01	0.06	0.08	0.01	0.03	0.06	0.01	0	0.01	0.11	0.02

Month

Figure 8.7 Chart with data table is used when the actual values are important to the reader

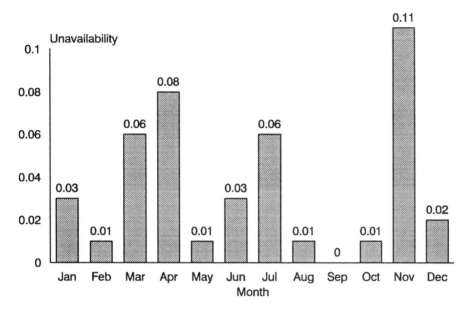

Figure 8.8 Chart with data values above each bar

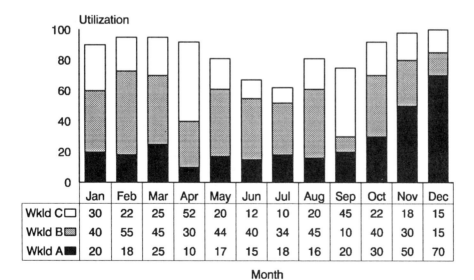

Figure 8.9 Stacked bar chart with data table

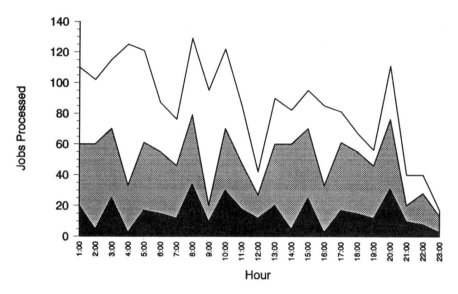

Figure 8.10 Use a stacked area chart for continuous data

Use a vertical bar chart to compare sets of data that change over time. For comparing data that do not involve time, use a horizontal bar chart.

Stacked bars are often used to show the parts of a total. For example, one may wish to show the workloads that comprise the total CPU utilization for discrete values (for example, hourly). Stacking gives the chart a stratified appearance (like layers of a cake). Since it is difficult to determine the values of any but the bottom layer of a stacked bar, it is better to include a data table (see Figure 8.9). Stacked bars should have as few components as possible (less than four for black and white).

For continuous data, a stacked area chart may be more desirable (see Figure 8.10). The stacked area chart is used to show changes in quantity, volume, or total. Put the series with the least variation on the bottom.

8.4 PIES, 3-D CHARTS, AND 3-D PIES

Although pie charts may appeal to journalists and marketing people by showing percentages of a total broken down into a few categories, they use a lot of ink for the amount of information provided. In addition, pie charts cannot be used to show time-series data (except maybe a "before" and "after" chart of two points in time). If you must use a pie chart (for example, to show what percentage of an expensive resource is used by what department), then limit the number of sections to six or less.

Some general guidelines for using pie charts effectively are:

- To emphasize a particular part of a whole, use a cut slice pie chart
- To reveal the breakdown of a part as another pie, use linked slice and pie
- To demonstrate the breakdown of a part as a column, use linked slice and column
- To show the relationship between sets of items that differ only in size use proportional pies

Avoid the use of 3-D charts in general—especially with pie charts. Pie charts become distorted by "tilting" and make it difficult for the reader to determine the true size of sections relative to one another.

It is difficult to determine the relative or true values of each category in a 3-D chart. Most graphics packages, with the exception of some scientific applications, actually just "create" the illusion of depth but provide no real z-axis. If there is considerable variability in the data, it may be difficult, even with chart perspective rotation, to find a view that does not hide data.

8.5   CHARTS SPECIFICALLY USED IN CAPACITY PLANNING

All data charts are comprised of two basic categories—pie charts and XY charts (also called Cartesian coordinate system charts). The data displayed are related by the dimensions of the chart. The first step in creating a chart is to determine the type of chart that will effectively represent the information. The following sections summarize the information best conveyed by each chart type and type of information.

8.5.1   Regression Analysis, Trends, and Curve Fitting

Regression analysis is a kind of curve fitting in that it fits the data with a function. It is the function, of course, which can be used to predict the future. Unfortunately, as a mathematical function, it will predict impossible data as well (for example, a negative Relative I/O Content—see Figure 8.11). In this example, a linear function was used and indicates a downward

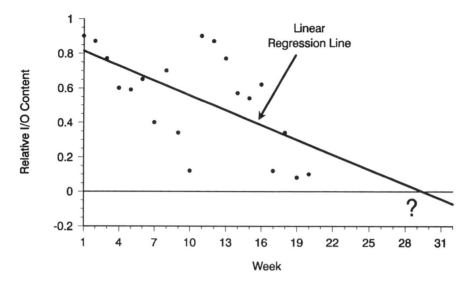

Figure 8.11 Regression line which predicts impossible data points

trend in RIOC. Since we know that computer systems do not experience
negative RIOC values (or even a zero value) and that RIOC will get smaller
as more power is consumed, the more realistic regression line could be
exponential (see Figure 8.12).

The important idea here is that the capacity planner needs to be aware
not only of the graphs and equations but must also understand the meaning
of the data. Clever graphs and precision mathematics should not replace
knowledge of the process and meaning of the data.

In my own experience with data charts, the following general guidelines
have been helpful (but they are only guidelines; you have to experiment a
little):

- *For time-series data* (to show change over time), the important features of
  the data are characterized by increase, decrease, rise, fall, highest, lowest, now, then, and fluctuation. Some guidelines for charting these
  attributes are:

  Bar Charts:

    —Use a vertical bar chart to show change over a few time periods

    —If titles are too long for x-axis, use a horizontal bar

    —For comparative totals for multiple sets of data, use a stacked bar

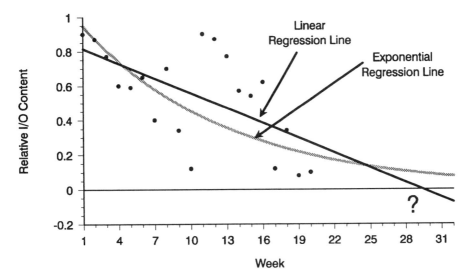

Figure 8.12 An exponential line provides a fit to that is more realistic

Line Charts:

—Use a line chart to show trends in data over time

—Make the most important line the thickest

—Show six or fewer lines (the fewer the better)

—Show estimates and projections as dashed or dotted line.

• *To demonstrate statistical patterns,* the important features of the data are the relationship of data to time or another variable, how one variable increases/decreases with or varies with another variable, or how one variable or function is linked to another. Some guidelines to follow are:

—To reveal trend for a single variable, use a line chart

—To show trend for a factor common to several variables, use a combined bar/line chart

—To represent a relationship between two separate changing items, use scatter points

—To display the relationship between several sets of changing items, use a scatter chart with markers

—To demonstrate trend, average, regression, frequency, or distribution, use a line chart

—For large changes in values where increments are on extremely different scales (for example, milliseconds and hours), use a logarithmic chart

—To represent a forecast pattern based on two sets of variables, use a regression line combined with scatter points

- *To represent order or rank of items,* the important features of the data are relationships such as more than, less than, equals, ranks, higher, lower, bigger, smaller, etc. To rank one variable compared to others, use a horizontal bar chart.

  When showing a trend line or regression line, either make it the only line on a chart with point values (dots) for the measured data or make the data being regressed visually different by combining different styles of lines (dotted, dashed, bold, light).

- *To illustrate relationships, correlations, or comparisons,* the important features of the data are such considerations as how many, how often, largest, least, most, smallest, etc. Some guidelines are:

  —For two closely related items, use an overlapping bar chart

  —For two sets of data about the same item, use a paired bar chart

  —For comparative totals for each set of data, use a stacked bar chart

  —To show emphasis on a particular factor, use a multiple line chart with contrast lines

  —To show emphasis on total quantities (e.g., volume) of several items, use stacked area charts

8.5.2 Demonstrating Statistical Measures

One of the significant capabilities of graphics is to demonstrate the range and shape of the data. The average (mean), for example, may not be a "typical value," especially when extreme values are present in the data series. Showing the average, minimum, and maximum helps to establish a feel for the range of values under consideration (see Figure 8.13).

As capacity planners become involved in service-level negotiations, the use of graphics is often helpful in demonstrating the appropriateness of certain measures of central tendency (mean or average, median, and mode). Managers may wish to use the "average" as a target for service-level objectives, unless they can see in a dramatic way that some other value (e.g., median) is more representative of the service actually being achieved. In Figure 8.14, no

Average Hourly Tape Mount Speed for Robotic Tape System

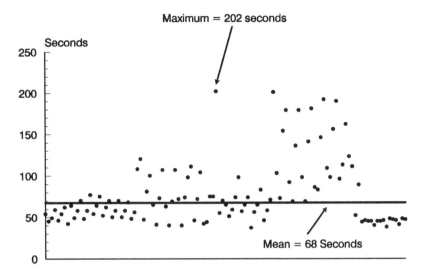

Figure 8.13 Use graphics to show important statistical measurements that occur in the data

Comparison of Mean and Median to Actual

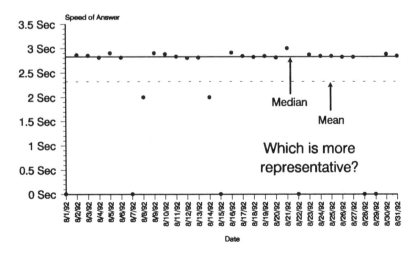

Figure 8.14 Comparing measures of central tendency may indicate that the "average" is not a "typical" value

actual measurement is even near the "average" value due to the occasional extreme values. In this case, we are looking at real data that measured the average speed of answer of a computerized telephone system. Note that the median is clearly more representative of actual service being experienced by the receivers of service.

8.5.3   Use of Goal Lines

Goal lines define a range of values that represent the goal within which you want your to data fall. The goal region can also represent a range of values that define the upper and lower limits of some measure of service.

Use a goal range when you want to compare your data with a specific range of values. In Figure 8.15, the goal area defines the minimum level of service (longest response time conditions) and the target level (acceptable response time) for an on-line system. The minimum level of service, in this case, is the upper limit (response time that is too slow). The target level of service (the performance standard) is the desired or acceptable level (a

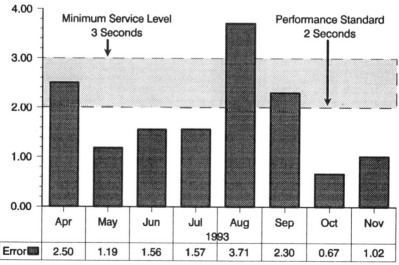

| Error | 2.50 | 1.19 | 1.56 | 1.57 | 3.71 | 2.30 | 0.67 | 1.02 |

Figure 8.15 Goal lines can be used to define a region of service levels

CPU Cluster Average Maximum Utilization by Week

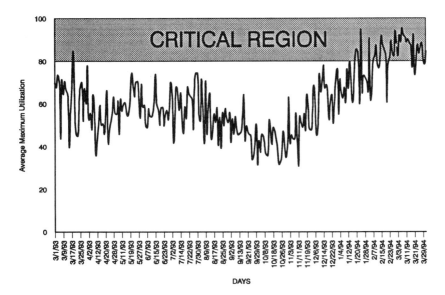

Figure 8.16 Use goal lines to define a critical region to alert the reader of alarming trends

lower value). Obviously, values that are better (lower) than the target are also very desirable. In reporting service-level measurements within the context of outsourced computer systems, it is critical to contract compliance to both in order to be able to report service and to make measurements of service clear and concise. Thus, the use of a goal range can clearly show when service is *within* acceptable bounds, *better* than acceptable (may earn award points or bonus points), or *unacceptable* (may cause penalties). Within a service-level context, it is desirable to have both a target to meet and a level at which exceptional service is defined.

For monitoring computer performance, the goal lines are commonly used to represent conditions that would impair the performance of the system and thus endanger service levels. In Figure 8.16, the data represent the average maximum weekly utilization for a DEC/VAX clustered system. As you can see, the system measurements have trended upwards into the critical region. This chart gives warning that system utilization is approaching levels that may become critical.

8.6   OBJECTS, SYMBOLS, AND INFORMATION

Because of the capacity planner's use of graphics, the ability to summarize large volumes of data into meaningful patterns, and familiarity in depth with computer technology, he or she is often called upon to illustrate concepts using symbols and objects. For example, an MIS executive may want to see the high-level relationships between computer systems, networks, and customers (see Figure 8.17). More common with capacity planners is the need to summarize the essential "big numbers" that characterize the total resources of a computer system (see Figure 8.18).

In this context, an *object* means any line, text, geometric shape, or symbol. For example, objects may be added to a chart (such as text annotations, voice annotations, polygons, rectangles, music, video, etc.). Graphic objects usually have the ability to be modified—for example, moved, copied, aligned, rotated, and/or filled with patterns, gradients, and bit maps.

In the world of graphics, *symbols* refer to images, clip art, or even other charts saved in a disk file. Many special symbol files come with graphics software. Some are available for special purposes (such as computer hard-

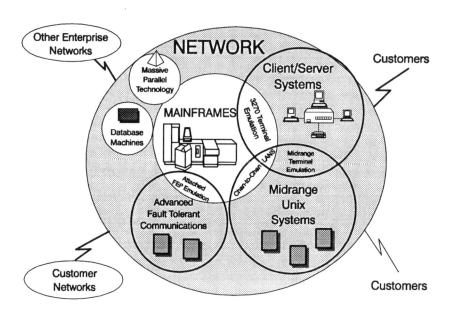

Figure 8.17 Graphics help summarize complex system relationships

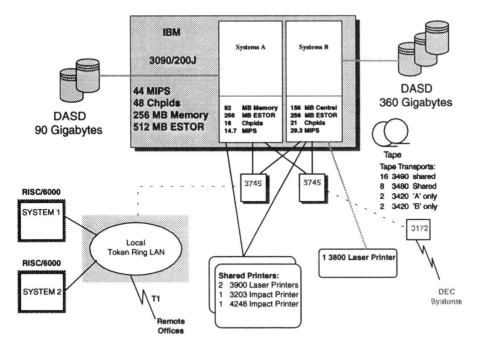

Figure 8.18 A summary of configuration information for a computer system should give the big picture

ware diagrams, flowcharting, etc.). If you have suitable drawing packages or a scanner, you can develop your own symbols.

There are few published guidelines for working with objects and symbols that can be targeted to MIS reporting. Generally, in my own experience, I have found the following to be useful:

- Avoid complexity. Too many items on a chart become confusing.

- Show only the big picture and avoid jargon unfamiliar or easily misunderstood by the reader. Use the terminology of the audience. Sacrifice precision for scope.

- Make sure you can read the text. Tiny fonts are not "cute." Avoid all uppercase—that gives the impression of shouting. Avoid "fancy" fonts. Avoid italics for small fonts.

- Use arrows to show connectivity if you have only a few connections. If you have many connections, use thin lines (see Figure 8.19).

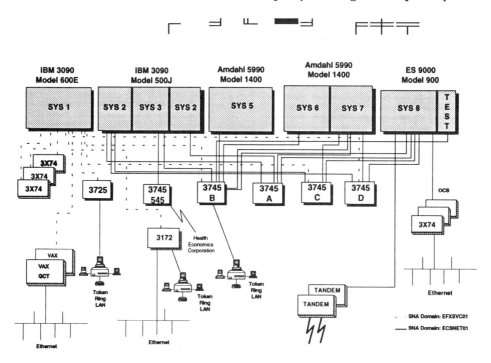

Figure 8.19 Many small lines can demonstrate complex connectivity considerations

- Try using drop shadows for boxes representing hardware. Then, within the boxes, use rectangles or squares to outline text representing software.

- In proposing system changes, show several alternative plans, including advantages and disadvantages and costs. Include the recommended plan but expect modifications. Eliminate from the charts technical detail that is not relevant to the issue.

As you begin to use graphics packages, you will discover successful techniques for combining symbols, objects, and data into effective presentations. (See Figure 8.20.) It is important to understand that although graphics software has the facility to greatly improve our ability to communicate information and reveal hidden patterns, it can also be used to complicate, confuse, and hide patterns. As you gain familiarity with graphics software, you will discover yourself "exploring" data series—not only with statistics but with graphics as well. This can be both exciting and rewarding.

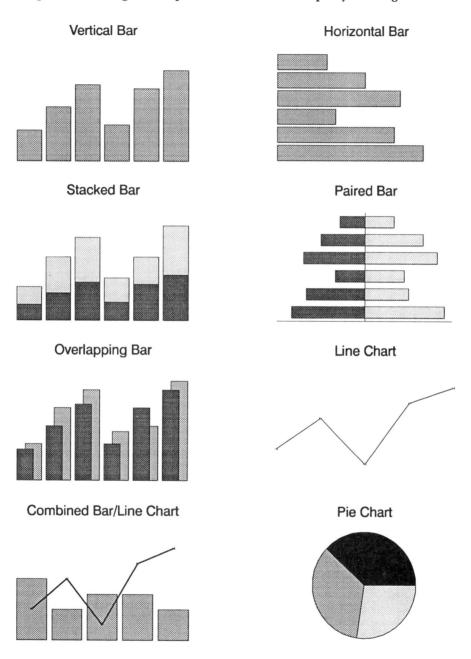

Figure 8.20 Various types of charts

Cut Slice

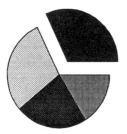

Linked Slice & Pie

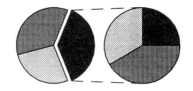

Proportional Pies

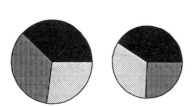

Scatter Points

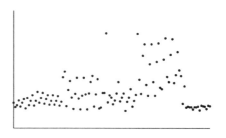

Scatter With Markers

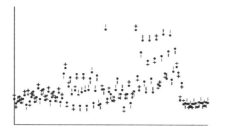

Logarithmic

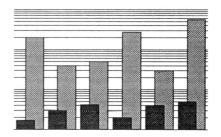

Figure 8.20   *(continued)*

8.7   REFERENCES

1. Pickover, Clifford A. *Computers, Pattern, Chaos and Beauty.* New York: St. Martin's Press, 1990, p. 10.

2. Jain, Raj. *The Art of Computer Systems Performance Analysis.* New York: John Wiley & Sons, 1991.

3. Finehirsh, Sidney. "Effective Service-Level Reporting." *CMG '85 Conference Proceedings*, 1985, pp. 505–509.

4. MacKinnon, Douglas R. "Is a Picture Always Worth a Thousand Words?" *CMG '87 Conference Proceedings*, 1987, pp. 272–278.

5. Powell, Calvin. "A Passion for Graphics Excellence." *CMG '88 Conference Proceedings*, 1988, pp. 761–765.

6. Schmid, Calvin F. *Statistical Graphics*, New York: John Wiley & Sons, 1983.

7. Tufte, Edward R. *The Visual Display of Quantitative Information.* Cheshire, CT: Graphics Press, 1983.

9

Systems Administration and the Future of Capacity Planning

9.1 SYSTEMS ADMINISTRATION

Capacity planning methodologies have evolved within the context of large systems administration and related systems management controls. Capacity planning as a process is responsive to the organizational context in which it functions and depending upon that context it may take on different administrative and control modalities. For example, at the operational level of an enterprise, capacity planning may be viewed as an exercise in applying the tools of extrapolative forecasting, resource optimization and other devices for effectively handling probabilistic outcomes. At higher levels, the capacity planning function may focus on ways to "manage" the human component of computer systems through a concentration on the adherence to planned resource levels determined via an audit process.

Capacity planning as a management control discipline is part of a body of techniques and procedures to plan, organize, operate, measure, and control information systems. In order to accomplish these objectives, IS management has evolved disciplines that form a framework for effective systems management. As computer systems evolved to accomodate the growing complexity of the information economy, the nature and issues of systems management have dramatically changed. Today's systems are increasingly moving towards multivendor, open, heterogeneous, client/server environments.

The application of systems management controls are continuting to evolve. System management strategies are process oriented and are focused on achieving consistent, workable, controllable and measurable results. Although these set of disciplines may vary from vendor to vendor and installation to installation, they can be generally summarized as follows:

9.1.1   Service-Level Management

Service-level management is the process of negotiating and defining the levels of service to be provided by the IS environment and includes the methods to measure, control, report, and manage IS systems. The objective is for the information systems environment and the receiver of services to understand service-level requirements, balance them against affordability, reach agreement on how those requirements will be fulfilled, and establish a documented agreement (the Service-Level Agreement).

Service-Level Agreements are used to determine capacity, which is defined as that level of resource utilization above which service levels cannot be met.

9.1.2   Problem Management

Problem management is the process of detecting, reporting, and correcting problems which can impact information system services. Typical areas would include hardware, software, communications, environmental factors and the procedures used by human beings within the information systems context. Capacity management may aid problem management by defining capacity limitations and the effects of computer system resource exhaustion.

9.1.3   Change Management

Change management is the process of planning, coordinating and monitoring changes which can impact information system services. These changes include system and network hardware, software, procedural, and environmental aspects of the total information system services function. As information systems grow in size and complexity, changes must be strictly controlled to avoid gross inefficiencies. The dominant driver, in large scale operations, is not mere economies of scale, it is managerial skill. A vital and essential managerial skill is an intolerance for unplanned, uncoordinated and surprise change.

Capacity management assists many of the planning and processing functions by defining plans for upgrades to system capacity. This includes early awareness of upcoming change activity. Change management is the vehicle for implementing capacity upgrades.

9.1.4 Performance Management

Performance management is the process of planning, defining, measuring, analyzing, reporting, and tuning the performance of information system resources including networks, hardware, operating systems, applications, and services. The objective of performance management is the effective application of procedures which optimize the use of systems resources while achieving committed user service levels.

Capacity management may identify absolute or transient capacity limitations which affect system performance. The long-term perspective of the capacity planning process assumes that performance ineffciencies are not intractable and will not be perpetuated into the future. The assumption for forecasting is that the present system and average states of the system over time represent a "reasonably" well-tuned environment.

Other categories for systems management functions may be focused on commonalities of interest within MIS or adherence to a common architecture. For example, systems automation management, batch management, online management, information asset management, business recovery management, and security management may be added to the list. Digital Equipment Corporation has outlined eight domains for system management [1] which are addressed in its Polycenter set of products and services. IBM promotes the SystemView framework for comprehensive management of open, distributed, heterogeneous enterprises [2].

9.2 NEW DIRECTIONS

A key issue for capacity planning, and many other systems management control disciplines, is this: How will the move toward distributed computing environments affect business and information systems platforms and architectures? The fundamental problems addressed by mature mainframe system management disciplines have not dramatically altered. However, the newly emerging disciplines differ from the old in a number of ways, including:

- the point of management and control
- the lack of acceptable performance/utilization metrics
- the new model of cooperative processing
- unknown workload and server characteristics
- cost

For capacity planning the shift is from precision to scope. Analytical modeling will not be feasible for the client/server environment. More likely, simulation modeling, benchmarking and baselining will be employed. As software/hardware vendors come to the market with better tools for measuring components, traditional capacity planning techniques will be utilized. Judgemental forecasting may become an interim modality as the opinion of experts becomes the court of last resort in predicting the behavior of complex distributed and networked systems.

The Gartner Group [3] has issued a convincing and comprehensive set of predictions regarding networked systems management and the new computing models:

- Best of breed in re-engineering will look for value improvement over cost improvement.

- Business demands during the 1990s will dramatically alter the nature of business transactions as well as all major components of the model.

- The new information technology platform will manifest itself first with organizational conflict and will mandate a new information technology architecture to enable the delivery of value.

- Client/server systems will be more expensive to operate than traditional, simple-platform systems.

- Distributed Computing is only one of the many forces contributing to the surge in the netoworked systems management market.

- Successful re-engineering will focus on exploiting new technology, not on leveraging or extending old technology.

- The thorny problems of creating a common representation of network and systems management resources will be solved via objects.

- A key challenge is for users to optimize placement of networked systems management services and applications.

- Systems integration will remain the linchpin of a successful networked systems management strategy until at least 1997.

The rapid evolution and deployment of the technical and functional capabilities of client/server systems has not yet provided users with the necessary structure to manage effectively the increased complexity and additional per-user costs of distributed client/server applications. These issues of systems management are critical because of the commitment to to client/server and to the heterogeneity that already exists in their environments. A modification of the distributed model, as a collection of isolated domains, may need modification in order to manage the entire enterprise. Most likely, a number of systems will need to cooperate in solving a particular systems management task. With this distributed server model, the ability to collect measurements from multiple platforms joined to a common network, will enable capacity management as an effective systems management discipline.

9.2.1 Systems Isomorphism and Business Elements

The new technologies of distributed computing may be closer in form, as a characteristic of system structure, to the information elements of the enterprise. By having data and function closer to the end users, plus the opportunity for end-user generated algorithmic processes, the "fit" between data, function status, and service delivery becomes more immediate. The metrics of workload classifications in client/server environments may very well be closely correlated to the business structure itself. The server-based model brings the management of processing intelligence down to where the users are, where the data is and where the bulk of the processing is taking place.

9.3 REFERENCES

1. Sinha, Prem S., "Redefining System Management." *CMG Transactions*, 82:69–72, Fall 1993.

2. Bernard, Karen, "Meeting The Systems Management Challenge," *CMG Transactions*, 82:73–78, Fall 1993.

3. Frank, Jeremy, "Key Disciplines for Distributed Network and Systems Management." Gartner Group Conference Presentation, Reader Notes, Spring 1994.

Appendix

A Brief Summary of Software Useful for Capacity Planners

This is a partial list of an enormous inventory of software that can be used for capacity planning for a variety of contexts. These are products that the author either has had experience with or has some knowledge of from product literature. More complete product descriptions and comparisons can be purchased, usually on a subscription basis, from a variety of companies, such as Datapro Information Services Group or The Institute for Computer Capacity Management.

The following list is in alphabetical order by software name.

athene

Metron Systems, Inc.
1559 Rockville Pike
Suite 408
Rockville, MD 20852
301-230-1810
Fax: 301-770-4097

Unisys A series, MCP, DEC, Pick, ICL, UNIX

Contact Vendor

An advanced capacity planning system combining data capture, workload analysis, service-level forecasting, computer-assisted model building, and integrated graphics. Data can be collected using snapshots. Analyzes CPU usage, I/O traffic, memory occupancy, and file utilization.

BEST/1

BGS Systems, Inc.
128 Technology Center
Waltham, MA 02254-9111
617-891-0000
Fax: 617-890-0000
VMS, UNIX, MVS, VM

Contact Vendor

A series of software products for modeling system performance. Supports such major capacity management functions as system description and calibration, performance prediction, and performance reporting. BEST/1-MVS supports IBM MVS environments; BEST/1-VMS supports DEC/VAX systems; BEST/1-VM supports IBM Virtual Machine Systems; BEST/1 For UNIX supports UNIX environments and uses HP's Performance Collection Software (PCS) to obtain UNIX performance measurement data in multivendor environments.

CA-ISS/THREE

Computer Associates International, Inc.
One Computer Associates Plaza
Islandia, NY 11788
800-225-5224
516-342-5224

IBM, MVS, PC-DOS, or MS-DOS

Contact Vendor

An integrated capacity management tool consisting of two major components: the MVS analyzer and the Capacity Planner. It assists in analyzing and eliminating capacity bottlenecks through comprehensive analytical modeling capabilities, advanced expert systems logic, and an extensive knowledge base with technical and financial information on processors, peripheral storage devices, and communication devices.

CAPACITY/Q™

Datametrics Systems Corp.
12150 East Monument Drive
Suite 300
Fairfax, VA 22033
800-869-3282
703-385-7700

IBM PC and compatibles

Contact Vendor

A microcomputer-based computer performance modeling tool. This is a generic package that applies to any computer system. Users enter input data via menu-driven form-fill screens. Provides detailed modeling of disk I/O subsystem components and modeling of disk features such as rotational position sensing. AUTO/Q provides interface between IBM's mainframe SMF/RMF performance data source and CAPACITY/Q.

CAPS™

Applied Computer Research, Inc.
P.O. Box 82266
Phoenix, AZ 85071-2266
800-234-2227
602-995-5929
Fax: 602-995-0905

IBM PC and compatibles, DOS

$1,450—permanent license
$485—one year rental.

Provides a beginning capacity plan with a high level of accuracy for a historical-based linear forecasting approach. Creates exhaust point forecasts of CPU, DASD, and network resources for any hardware platform.

DECperformance Solution™ (DECps)

Digital Equipment Corp.
Contact local branch.

DEC, VAX, VMS

Contact Vendor

DECps is an integrated set of performance and capacity management facilities that incorporates the existing VAX Performance Advisor and the Software Performance Monitor for evaluating and optimizing system resources. Consisting of four components, DECps includes: (1) DECperformance Solution Data Collector—gathers VMS system data and provides archiving; (2) DECperformance Solution Performance Advisor—provides performance analysis using expert system capabilities and generates reports and graphics to provide a statistical overview of system performance; (3) DECperformance Solution Capacity Planner—uses analytic modeling techniques to determine system performance for various workloads and configurations—useful for scenario evaluation and saturation analysis; (4) DECperformance Solution Accounting Chargeback—allocates charges for resource usage and generates extensive reports.

Explicit MVS Mainframe Capacity Planner (MCP)

Technetronic, Inc.
1111 Prince of Wales Drive
Reston, VA 22091
800-533-5128
703-264-8000
Fax: 703-264-1312

IBM PC/AT, PS2, 370, 30XX, 43XX, ES/9000 and compatibles, MVS/ESA, MVS/XA, MVS/SP

Contact Vendor

Uses network queuing theory and mean value analysis techniques to model the performance of MVS computer installations and solve system management problems. Optional components can predict the effect on an I/O subsystem of a conversion from MVS/SP to MVS/XA and can model changes to I/O topology, reorganizing DASD, memory modeling, response time distributions, and queue distributions.

Forecast/3000 Capacity Planner

Lund Performance Solutions
3111 Santiam Highway
Suite I
Albany, OR 97321
503-926-3800
Fax: 503-926-7723
IBM PC or compatible

Contact Vendor

A queuing network modeling system that can be used to predict future hardware requirements or the effects of application changes. Provides full-color graphics and window menus. Calculates and reports current and future response times, utilizations, and throughput for user-defined workloads.

HP RXForecast

Hewlett-Packard
1501 Page Mill Road
Palo Alto, CA 94303
415-857-1501

H-P

$3,400

Uses data generated by HP LaserRX software for projections of system resource requirements, including CPU usage, response time, and disk I/O.

Users can select forecast adjustments for seasonal variations. Uses several statistical algorithms and reports forecast validity. Can include the use of confidence-level lines and threshold lines on graphs.

iMETRICS

Compumetrics, Inc.
Suite 600
7 Dey Street
New York, NY 10007
800-335-7516
212-346-7569
Fax: 212-346-7568

IBM PC or compatibles

Contact Vendor

Provides service-level information, graphic profiles, trend displays, what-if analyses, distribution summaries, and exception displays for IBM MVS systems, IBM AS/400 systems, DASD, TSO, CICS, SNA, and VM. Runs under Microsoft Windows. Excellent graphics and exception reporting. Data are downloaded from mainframe systems.

ISM/CP™ Base

The Info. Systems Manager Inc.
301 Broadway
Bethlehem, PA 18015
215-865-0300
Fax: 215-868-6277

IBM, MVS/370, MVS/XA, MVS/ESA

$3,500 initial fee plus $1,000

This is a combination software/service. The service provides monthly reports, more than 40 color charts, and a PC-based software system that is preloaded with customer data compiled from RMF.

The PC System supplements these charts with detailed information, combined with more than 100 analysis and modeling functions. Analysis tools are provided for capacity planning activities, including analyzing the growth of workloads, estimating new workloads, and estimating latent demand. Performance analysis tools include analysis on the processor complex, real storage, the paging subsystem, and the I/O subsystem.

Modeling and forecasting functions are provided throughout the PC System. Modeling tools enable the user to build a capacity plan by selecting processor upgrades as appropriate and by forecasting the impact of proposed system changes in the areas of CPU, real and expanded storage, the paging subsystem, the I/O subsystem, and workloads.

The product includes PR/SM support, SCP support in the processor modeling functions, and support in the I/O subsystem modeling functions for non-IBM devices.

MAP

Amdahl Corp.
1250 East Arques Avenue MS215
Sunnyvale, CA 94086
408-746-6000

Amdahl, IBM and plug-compatibles, Burroughs (Unisys), Hewlett-Packard, DEC

Contact Vendor

A modeling and analysis package using analytic techniques to predict the effects that workload growth, upgrades, and configuration changes may have on system performance.

Data for the model can be automated for machine-readable data or entered manually.

MICS Capacity Planner

Legent Corporation
114 Turnpike Road
Westboro, MA 01581
800-676-5468
508-836-5952
Fax: 508-836-5992

IBM 370, 30XX, 43XX, and compatibles; MVS, MVS/XA, MVS/ESA

Contact Vendor

Addresses the two key areas of capacity planning: workload characterization and workload forecasting. Workload characterization uses data from the MICS database. Using current work activity, it helps establish a baseline for workloads.

Aids in the identification of statistically representative resource demand patterns.

Workload forecasting is aided by the provision of five techniques as well as graphics presentations. The techniques include profile and trending, simple regression, univariate modeling, multivariate regression, and business element forecasting.

Twelve standard applications (CPU, DASD, CICS, MVS/XA, MVS/ESA, VM, VM/XA, LPAR (PR/SM), DB2, IMS, Workload, and SNA).

MOGUL™—Model Generator with User Lead-Through

High Performance Software
4288 Upham Road
Dayton, OH 45429
513-294-5558

IBM, PC-DOS, UNIX

Contact Vendor

MOGUL is used for building simulation models of computer systems and communication networks, supporting both high-level model design and a high degree of detail. System components, including processors, communication links, and peripheral devices, are chosen from a group of predefined types by using menus and screens. A process flow graph is then entered through a MOGUL editor to create the activity paths in the model.

MXG™ Merrill's Expanded Guide to CPE Using the SAS™ System

Merrill Consultants
10717 Cromwell Drive
Dallas, TX 75229-5112

214-351-1966
Fax: 214-350-3694

IBM, MVS, VM, DOS

$1,300/site first year;
$500/year thereafter.

MXG is an integrated collection of hundreds of SAS programs that extract information from the raw measurement records created by the MVS, VM, and DOS operating systems and their subsystems. Merrill's Expanded Guide executes as an SAS application and will create a Performance Data Base. This database is an SAS data library, which is used for the analysis and reporting of performance objectives, for system tuning, and for capacity measurement and management.

The MXG GUIDE provides information on computer performance analysis, including database, availability, and workload analyses; tape drive utilization; and print requirements; as well as accounting, benchmarking, capacity measurement, establishing the CPE organization, variability of CPU measures, grouping and measuring CICS response, and differences between MVS/370 and MVS/XA SMF and RMF data.

myriad™

PALLAS International Corp.
1763 Valhalla Court
San Jose, CA 95132
408-923-5509

IBM PC/AT/XT, PS/2, and compatibles; DOS 2.0

Single license: $995. Unlimited copy site license available.

A modeling system that include five groups of models:

1. Probability distributions, including many important discrete and continuous distributions, as well as general inequalities; percentile computation is included for continuous distributions.
2. Simple infinite queues, such as M/M/1, M/G/1, GI/M/1, M/M/c, M/G/1 with priorities, etc.

3. Simple finite queues, such as M/M/c/K, machine repair models, loss systems, etc.

4. Networks of queues, including a central server model of multiprogramming, a model of a multiprogrammed interactive system with memory constraints, and open tandem networks with finite buffers and blocking.

5. Special models, including such important models as a multiclass loss system, an original model of bandwidth sharing, a model of Token Ring LAN, or an Ethernet model.

Solution depends on the model: exact or proven approximate analysis or discrete-event simulation.

OptiModel™

Legent Corporation
(see previous entry under MICS Capacity Planner)

IBM PC and compatibles, MVS/XA, MVS/ESA

Contact Vendor

OptiModel is a PC-based modeling system that can model workload changes, analyze system performance, display detailed activity reports and color graphs, and create files to be used with PC presentation software. For capacity planning, OptiModel helps to address these issues:

1. The life expectancy of equipment
2. What resources need to be upgraded and when
3. The most cost-effective equipment solutions
4. Data center consolidation
5. Software architectures

Supports the use of scenario analysis; allows multiple systems in the same model for determining data center consolidations or the separation of logical/physical systems.

PACE—Performance Analysis/Capacity Evaluation Subsystem

The Adesse Corp.
36 Mill Plain Road
Suite 307
Danbury, CT 06811
203-790-9473

IBM 370, 303X, 308X, 3090, 43XX, and plug-compatibles; VM/SP

$22,500+/CPU; $975/month; $225/month maintenance.

Uses a strategy of running benchmarks to perform various evaluations.
PACE measures the response times that characterize system performance
and reports them on demand using a full-screen display. Incorporates
several utilities that are helpful during and after benchmarks: (1) Transaction Simulator—can be used to simulate transactions that might occur in
a typical workload, (2) Workload Simulator—can simulate the activity of
an entire virtual machine, and (3) Session Log Viewer—permits PACE
session screen logs to be reviewed after a run is complete.

PILOT

Axios Products, Inc.
1373-10 Veterans Highway
Hauppauge, NY 11788
800-877-0990
516-979-0100
Fax: 516-979-0537

For PILOT/CICS or PILOT/MVS: IBM mainframes, PC/AT/XT, and
compatibles; MVS, MVS/XA
PILOT/SMF: IBM, MVS
PILOT/CICS or PILOT/MVS—$9,000;
PILOT/SMF—$10,000.

Used for performance tuning and capacity planning for CICS and MVS
environments.

PILOT/CICS is a reporting, tracking, and modeling component that utilizes statistics and graphs to provide information on the consumption of CICS resources and CICS transaction rates. PILOT/CICS works with Lotus 1-2-3 to model the CICS environment and provide forecast analysis. Of interest to capacity planners is the PILOT/CICS simulator, which provides an interactive tool for capacity planning and performance analysis of complex on-line environments. The PILOT/CICS simulator is a modifiable model, which answers questions such as what would happen in a particular environment with different CPUs, dispatching priorities, disks, main storage, etc.

The PILOT/MVS component analyzes, tracks, and makes predictions regarding MVS and MVS/XA environments. Numerous metrics are provided for MVS, DASD, TSO, and I/O.

PILOT/SMF is an all-purpose migration, performance, audit, and accounting tool. It provides special modules to format SMF records and better manage SMF data.

PlanWare

Communications Programming Inc.
180 North LaSalle
Suite 2920
Chicago, IL 60601
708-386-9676
Fax: 708-383-1051

IBM PC and compatibles, Lotus 1-2-3

$495

A set of tools for determining hardware requirements using modeling techniques. Runs under Lotus 1-2-3 and uses Lotus macro programming facilities extensively.

Includes a number of preprogrammed reports. These include spreadsheet table summary lists and bar or pie chart graphics.

QASE® RT

Advanced System Technologies
12200 East Briarwood Avenue
Suite 260
Englewood, CO 80112
303-790-4242
Fax: 303-790-2816

Apple MacIntosh

QASE RT/91—$4,900
QASE RT/S—$9,800

A system-level CASE tool that enables users to describe and analyze a complex computer system. Combines use of CASE specification tools, performance modeling, and simulation languages. Used for designing real-time and distributed systems and for comparing design alternatives.

The QASE RT's object types provide descriptions of hardware, software, and data and include the following features:

- Workloads are deterministic or probabilistic events and data that stimulate the system.
- Stimulus control flow drawings show the logical system functions that respond to workload events.
- Hardware drawings show the interconnections of processing, storage, and communication devices.
- Data are represented by logical data elements, stores, and flows.
- Operating systems and communications protocols define overhead and scheduling disciplines.
- Allocation strategies (software modules to processors and data stores to storage devices) are independent from the logical function descriptions.

SAS System

SAS Institute Inc.
SAS Campus Drive
Cary, NC 27513-2414

919-677-8000
Fax: 919-677-8123

IBM 370, 390, 30XX, 43XX, 937X, PS/2, PC/AT, and compatibles; OS, MVS, TSO, CMS, DOS/VSE, MS-DOS, PC/DOS, OS/2, Windows, Windows NT; DEC VAX; VMS; Data General Eclipse MV; AOS/VS; Prime 50; PRIMOS; UNIX Workstations from Sun, HP, DEC, IBM, Data General, MIPS, Solbourne, Convex, SGI, NeXT, and Apollo; SunOS, HP-UX, RISC/ULTRIX, Convexos, IRIX, NeXTStep, AIX, DG/UX, RISC/OS, and DOMAIN/OS.

Contact Vendor

SAS is probably the most popular of all capacity planning tools—it is the Latin of Capacity Planning Theology. The SAS system is an integrated suite of software products, which includes capabilities for spreadsheets, graphics, data analysis, report writing, quality improvement, project management, computer performance evaluation, client/server computing, database access, decision support, applications development, and more. It is used extensively by capacity planners because of its ability to manipulate and analyze machine-readable resource consumption measurement data and its ability to perform advanced statistical analyses.

SCERT

See entry for Athene

IBM, PC 370/AT

Perpetual license—$49,500

SCERT is a performance management tool that projects how workloads will perform in hardware, software, and communications environments. Features provide choice in model development, report formats, and detail level.

Includes a performance characteristics library, which contains simulation-ready models of major hardware and control software systems, including CPU, memory, channels, peripherals, communications networks, operating systems, and languages.

Mathematical models representing the workload and computer resources are manipulated by a set of algorithms to determine how the system would perform.

The applications library allows the user to access prebuilt workload models, configuration models, and macro models (such as CICS or IDMS) and incorporate them (with or without modification) directly into the SCERT process.

SES/Client/Server Performance Modeler

Scientific and Engineering Software
4301 Westbank Drive
Bldg. A
Austin, TX 78746
512-328-5544
Fax: 512-327-6646

Sun SPARC, HP 9000 Model 700, IBM RS/6000, DEC ULTRIX

Contact Vendor

A simulation model for client/server systems. Allows users to evaluate the performance tradeoffs of multiple scenarios by varying such components as network type and topology, data storage distributions, hardware configurations, processing bottlenecks, etc. Includes on-screen animation to view how transactions traverse the model with breakpoints and tracing. Reports include predefined statistics, including mean, minimum, maximum, and standard deviation, for a range of performance characteristics. Output from the model is easy to use with standard spreadsheet formats.

VAM™/Perspective

Zitel Corporation
47211 Bayside Parkway
Fremont, CA 94538
510-440-9600

IBM PC, Windows

Contact Vendor

A simulation tool that utilizes an expert system component to analyze system capacity. Uses pull-down menus and dialog boxes to simplify the analysis process. Provides both transaction and batch process modeling.

Vizualize

ESI
3200 Commonwealth Boulevard
Tallahassee, FL 32303
904-575-0179

Unisys A, V

Contact Vendor

A performance and capacity planning workstation for Unisys A and V series. Projects capacity based on resource growth. Analysis is PC based.

Glossary

The terminology of capacity planning is immense. This glossary is limited to some of the more common terms you will encounter in doing capacity planning. Some of the terms are unique to capacity planning, but many overlap in their meanings with special applications of statistical modeling.

In capacity planning, familiar words take on unfamiliar meanings. Some words seem to mean something very different compared to other computer disciplines. For example, the word *normalization* has a specific meaning in capacity planning that is distinctly different from the same word when used in the context of relational database technology; *MAD* does not mean angry, but *Mean Absolute Deviation*; and *life expectancy* refers not to how long someone will live but to *how long a system or any resource will last.*

Many of the definitions in this glossary are highly simplified. This was done in order to avoid lengthy mathematical expressions as, for example, in statistical concepts. If you need a more formal definition of statistical terms, consult a statistics reference book. For an expanded definition of capacity planning terminology, read the section of this book where the term is explained.

Access density The propensity of disk-resident data to result in disk I/Os as the workload is being processed.

Acquired-Objective-Analysis An intellectual posture, which is focused on analyzing trends or patterns from the past with the expectation that these historical patterns will develop in the future as well.

Adaptive filtering Any of several time-series forecasting models that update their parameters continuously in an attempt to follow changes in the data.

Adaptive response rate   A variation of exponential smoothing in which the algorithm determines the value of the smoothing constant at any given time, based on the error.

Additive seasonality   A trend-seasonal pattern in which the magnitude of the seasonal fluctuations remains constant regardless of the level of the data. As demand increases over time, the relative height of the seasonal peaks remains the same if this type of pattern is present.

Analysis and projection   The use of modeling or simulation tools and statistical analysis of the measurement data and business element processing volumes to forecast future growth and the impact on computer resources of new applications.

Analysis of variance (ANOVA)   A statistical procedure to test the significance of the results of other procedures, such as linear regression. ANOVA tells you whether a significant amount of the variation in your data is explained by the model that you are using.

Analytic forecasting   Forecasting activity that utilizes mathematical methods to identify trends or causal patterns.

ANOVA   An abbreviation for analysis of variance.

AOA   Abbreviation for Acquired-Objective-Analysis.

Architecture   The design of a system or process. Architectural considerations are often a critical dimension in determining system capacity.

Autocorrelation (AC)   In time-series data, the correlation between successive data values. If autocorrelation is present, the data must be described by an autoregressive (AR) model.

Autocorrelation coefficient   Represents the strength of association between successive values of the same variable.

Automatic initiation manager (AIM)   A systems-managed storage product.

Autoregressive (AR) model   A time-series regression model that describes the relationship between a dependent variable and several of its past values, each of which is assigned a weight. Used when significant autocorrelation is present.

Autoregressive integrated moving average model (ARIMA) The model used for a nonstationary, nonseasonal time series that contains both AR (autoregression) and MA (moving average) parameters. Before the ARIMA model can be used, the data must be differenced to achieve stationarity.

Award points A common nomenclature used to describe the evaluation of MIS in exceeding performance objectives relative to a service-level contract.

Batch initiators In MVS, initiators provide pathways into the system for batch (background) work.

Best linear unbiased estimators (BLUE) In regression analysis, coefficients derived by least squares.

Bias This indicates that some factor causes estimates used in forecasting to be consistently higher or lower than they should be. For example, if the capacity planner wanted to determine the average on-line response time for an application, but only measured the application during the middle of the night when few people were on the system, the results would be biased.

Binomial distribution A distribution that describes data that is characterized with the presence or absence of some attribute.

Block size A grouping of records into blocks is called the *block size*. The cylinder and track use of a file depend on the block size of the file and type of disk on which it resides.

Box-Cox transformations A set of transformations designed to make the relationship between two variables linear.

Box-Jenkins technique A method for selecting the model that best fits a given set of time-series data. The three basic types of models considered are the AR (autoregressive), MA (moving average), and ARMA (autoregressive moving average).

Business element A unit of measure used in business, from business terminology, that is used for planning purposes.

Business unit A business element.

CA-1   A tape management systems product that is the most popular system available today. It is from Computer Associates. Originally named Tape Management System (TMS), the product was written in 1971. CA-1 allows a storage manager to define life cycles for each tape, and when the specified number of cycles has passed, CA-1 automatically scratches the tape. A nice feature of CA-1 is that cycles can be set up by absolute numbers or by specific dates.

CA-ASM2   One of several Computer Associates products for systems-managed storage that helps storage managers and capacity planners in analyzing the current data storage environment.

Caching   Caching works as a high-speed, solid-state intermediary between a storage device, generally disk or cartridge tape, and a system requesting data. When a read request is sent to the disk, the cache intercepts it. The system checks to see if it has already accessed this data, and, if it has, it sends it back to the system from the cache (which is much faster).

Capacity management   Those activities associated with managing current system capacity as compared to future system capacity.

Categorical data   Data that fall into several categories, instead of a continuous scale. For example, measures of service may be grouped into several different categories, such as minimum service level, service-level target, and above target.

Causal forecasting   Forecasting methods in which elements that directly cause increase or decrease in computer resource consumption are analyzed, simulated, or modeled.

Causal models   Models used to forecast data in which the predictor variable(s) represents something other than time. Natural forecasting unit techniques use this approach.

Causal reconstruction   The explanation of past system behavior using causal models that can then be applied to future systems behavior.

Central tendency   A way of measuring the typical or expected value for a set of data. Measures of central tendency include the mean (average), median (middle), and mode (most frequently occurring).

Centroid method In the *centroid* method of cluster analysis, the distance between two clusters is defined as the squared Euclidean distance between their means.

Change management Change management is the process of planning, co-ordinating, and monitoring changes that can impact information system services. These changes include system and network hardware, software, procedural, and environmental aspects of the total information system services function.

Cluster analysis Cluster analysis is a statistical technique that helps develop categories for the classification of data in groups. For example, it may be used to determine appropriate job class structures by exploiting the natural patterns of resource requirements in the workload. It is an iterative process in which clusters are successively approximated.

Coefficient A number or symbol used as a multiplier of a variable. Also used to refer to statistical parameters, such as the correlation coefficient or the coefficient of variation.

Coefficient of determination The formal name for the square of the correlation coefficient. It is used in causal forecasting models, such as natural forecasting unit models or business element models, as a measure of the percentage of variation in the Y variable, which is explained or determined by variation in the X variable.

Coefficient of variation A parameter calculated by taking the standard deviation of a set of data and dividing it by the mean. The result is used as an index of the amount of variation in the data. Since it is relative to the mean, this statistic may be used to compare sets of data that have considerably different scales or dimensions, for example, the variation in response times in milliseconds compared to the variation in batch throughput in hours.

Competitive benchmarking A technique that compares the performance of data centers to determine the best practice and to establish and validate process goals for process improvement.

Computer resource unit A composite measure of resource consumption that combines the use of individual resources into a single value.

Confidence interval   A "plus or minus" factor used to bracket an estimate, often based on some multiple of the standard deviation.

Confidence level   The level of confidence you have in your forecast. Statisticians may use the 95 percent confidence level, but sometimes the 90 or 99 percent level is used instead.

Correlation   A statistically significant association between two variables; i.e., if two events or processes are correlated, then a change in one of them tends to be associated with a change in the other. This does not imply that one event causes the other, nor does it explain the reason for the association.

Correlation coefficient (R)   A value calculated to determine whether or not two variables are correlated. The square of R is the coefficient of determination.

Covariance   A parameter that reflects the degree to which two variables tend to vary together.

Curve fitting   A process of fitting a line to data using an equation. For example, the straight line that best fits a series of data is determined using simple time-series regression. Least-square regression can also be used for lines that are not straight. The coefficient of determination—computing this value is one step in computing the regression—will also tell you how well the curve fits the data.

Curvilinear regression   A regression model in which the line that best fits the data is nonlinear rather than linear.

Cybernetic control model   A control model for service objective and control that utilizes feedback mechanisms.

Cyclic data   Another word for seasonal data, because seasons represent one type of cyclic pattern. Statisticians may distinguish between cyclic and seasonal components of time-series data, in which case cyclic patterns are long-term fluctuations with a period of one to twelve years, and seasonal patterns occur within a year and are often equivalent to quarterly patterns. The cyclic patterns of the enterprise, as drivers of workloads, are the primary focus of capacity planning.

Cylinder   Unlike geometry, this also refers to a group of tracks on a disk drive

Data   From a mathematical perspective, data are the values of a variable.

From a capacity planning perspective, data are bits of information that take up storage resources, are processed by programs (I/O data), and turned into more data (processed into informational presentations), backed up, archived, stored, and so forth. Data become information when they have been rearranged or manipulated in such a way that they tell you something that you want to know.

Data class   A classification of storage used in systems-managed storage. In the data class parameters, the storage administrator sets up the physical data set characteristics, such as record length, space, data set organization, and block size. These record characteristics are passed on to a data set at allocation time, based on the low-level qualifier in the data set name.

Data compression   This usually means running data through a program that takes out irrelevant information, such as spaces, thereby squeezing a lot more relevant data in smaller areas. Depending on the data being compressed, organizations can see an 80 percent reduction in space requirements, especially in their tape backups.

There are drawbacks to data compression, however. Compression can actually degrade response time when used for certain disk-based applications.

Data remoteness factor (DRF)   DRF represents the ratio of on-line DASD resident data gigabytes to the main storage resident gigabytes.

Data transfer time   In IBM large systems environments, the time required to transfer the data between the disk storage and central storage is the data transfer time. For a 4- to 6-Kbyte record, this averages about 1 to 2 milliseconds. It is one component of connect time.

Data transformation   Any process that converts data, in a systematic manner, to new data, usually for the purposes of scaling. For example, if you wish to use time as a predictor variable in a forecast equation, you must first convert the months to numbers. Data values also can be converted to a common scale such as CPU normalization transformations (for CPU time from systems of different speeds).

Decomposition technique   A forecasting technique to break down a time series into the following components: trend, seasonal, cyclical, and irregular.

Defactualized model A forecast model that replaces fact with opinion, intuition, feelings, etc.

Delphi method A judgmental technique in which participating experts respond to a series of reiterated written questionnaires. The objective of the Delphi method is to reduce the variance of response from the experts so that a decision can be made with some degree of unanimity.

Dependent variable The *Y* variable in a regression model. The name results from the fact that, in a causal model, the value of *Y* is considered to *depend* on the value of the *X* variable(s).

DFDSS Data Facility Data Set Services, an IBM product, is part of a systems-managed storage environment which, as a companion to DFHSM, performs the actual data set moves.

DFHSM Data Facility Hierarchical Storage Manager, an IBM product that is part of a systems-managed storage strategy. DFHSM handles the data backup and recovery functions and controls migrating inactive data sets to other storage media.

Disk pooling A technique of aggregating disk storage volumes, which enables the storage manager to keep like data on a given set of disk packs. For example, companies may have a production pool of ten disks, a test pool of five disks, and a temporary pool of ten disks. Pooling disks in this way aids in allocating and managing data on a day-to-day basis, as well as making it easier for a capacity planner to evaluate current capacity.

Dispersion The amount of variation in a set of data—for example, variance, the standard deviation, and the mean absolute deviation.

DMS/OS One of several tools available to help storage managers and capacity planners in analyzing the DASD environment. DMS/OS is from Sterling Software. With DMS/OS, a storage manager or capacity planner can perform exception analyses, check on the active files, and automatically archive those that are inactive.

Empirical Based on observation rather than speculation or theory.

Execution states The status of an address space or program, such as active, idle, delayed, contention, etc.

Execution time   This is the time that a program is actually running (doing work) in the system as compared to time spent waiting for I/Os, paging, or other similar events that are external to the program.

Exogenous variable   Refers to a variable that depends only on variables that are outside the system that the forecast model represents.

Explanatory model   A causal model.

Exponential growth   A pattern of increase that fits the model $y = 2^2$. The graph curves sharply upward.

Exponential smoothing   A time-series technique in which the forecast for the next interval is based on a weighted average of the data for the previous n intervals. The weight is highest for the most recent interval, whereas those for earlier intervals decrease exponentially.

Exterior resource consumption   This is a measure of resources external to the central processing unit and memory, such as tape drives, disk mounts, forms changes, etc.

F value statistic   A measure used to compare two variances, to see whether there is a statistically significant difference between them.

File naming conventions   File naming conventions play an important role in evaluating the current disk capacity. Storage managers and capacity planners need to know if data are temporary or permanent, test or production, system or user. Having naming standards that categorize data by use and ownership criteria makes measurement and forecasting possible.

Filter   The filter is a test that looks at each forecast to see how different it is from the actual data value, once the latter is known. If the forecast is off by more than a specified amount, the result is called a *filter trip* (like tripping an alarm). Then you have a situation where the filter notifies you that the forecast is outside the limits you have set.

Final forecast   A mathematical forecast is combined with the judgment of a manager or other decision maker. If the two are at odds, this can be extremely problematic.

Footprint This refers to how much phsycial space (usually in a raised-floor computer room) some device takes up. The ideal hardware has immense capacity within a tiny footprint.

Forecast Any attempt to predict future events.

Full track blocking A method of aggregating data records into blocks that exploit the DASD track size. Due to the relationship of the I/O access methods in the operating system and the storage device geometry, "full track" blocking techniques greatly improve I/O performance and reduce "wasted" space.

Generalized adaptive filtering (GAF) A version of adaptive filtering that incorporates the concept of autocorrelation.

Generalized least squares (GLS) The process of transforming data and then applying ordinary least squares analysis to the transformed data.

Geometric growth A pattern of increase that fits the general model $y = x^2$. Instead of being an exponent, as in exponential growth, X has an exponent. The graph curves sharply upward but not as rapidly as in exponential growth.

Geometric mean (geometric average) To find the geometric average of a series of numbers, either (1) find their logarithms, calculate the mean of these values, and then transform the result back to an ordinary number by finding its antilogarithm; or (2) multiply together all n values in the series and then find the nth root of the product.

Harmonic series A time series that involves two trigonometric functions: the sine and the cosine.

Heterogeneity Referring to mixed architectures, proprietary and open, including multiple vendors, that are increasingly typical in large business enterprises employing computer systems.

Heuristics Guidelines. When used in service-level administration, they are statements of service-level targets that are used for control actions within MIS in order to support more public or formal statements of service

Homoscedastic Describes a variable for which the variance is the same across the range of observed values.

Horizontal distribution Horizontal data tend to have a constant average value despite variation within the individual data values. Not much change from one forecast interval to the next. Because of the near constant average values, this distribution is also called stationary, or flat.

IMA Abbreviation for Integrated Moving Average.

Integrated moving average (IMA) model The model used in time-series analysis for a nonstationary, nonseasonal series that contains only moving average parameters. Before the IMA model can be used, the data must be differenced to achieve stationarity.

Interval forecast A forecast that includes a confidence interval, as in the following statement: "The expected tape mount volume in April is 28,382 plus or minus 658."

Intuitive-subjective-synthesis An intellectual posture, which focuses on the intuitive ability to understand the human activities within the organization and discern which events are likely to transpire.

IOSQ time In MVS systems, refers to the time that the I/O supervisor (IOS) waits for a DASD device to become free.

Isomorphic As applied to general systems properties, meaning similar in form.

ISS Abbreviation for Intuitive-Subjective-Synthesis.

JCL Job Control Language. Typically associated with IBM large systems. A parametric language invented by IBM to strike terror in the hearts of programmers and wreak havoc on algorithmic thinking. JCL is nonrecursive, highly symbolic, and tediously descriptive of the program operating environment and associated files.

Job classes For MVS batch processing, job classes are used to categorize the type of work to be processed. What the categories are is completely arbitrary, for example, "Jobs that mount three or more tapes" or "Jobs that Sally runs on Saturdays".

Judgmental forecasting Forecasting that is primarily intuitive and looks at historical milestones and patterns of human behavior in the organization as well as in the marketplace in which the business functions.

Jury of executive opinion A judgmental forecasting method, and probably the most common in use, in which a group of managers holds a meeting to arrive at a consensus forecast or at least a forecast that is acceptable to the highest ranking manager present.

Latent demand Latent demand is the demand on the system that is not being serviced due to restrictions of existing system capacity or the limitations of the application software. New resources may unleash this pent-up demand and consume the excess capacity in such a way that resource exhaustion takes place much faster than expected.

Life expectancy In capacity planning, it is how long a system or any system resource will last.

Logical resource The virtual objects and their composite structures, such as page size, addressability, etc.

Lumpy data A pattern of data values that fluctuates over a wide range from one interval to another but which shows no evidence of a predictable seasonal pattern.

MAD Abbreviation for Mean Absolute Deviation.

Mean absolute deviation (MAD) The mean absolute deviation (MAD) is a method for estimating variation. Although not as good an estimator as the standard deviation, it is easily comprehended by those less inclined to statistical sophistication. You find the absolute value of the difference between each actual measurement and the forecast amount. Then, the mean of these differences is used as an indicator of the variation between forecast and actual. If this value is very high, management's evaluation of the capacity planner's ability to forecast might be correspondingly low.

Measurement base Data that provide information on current configuration and resource use.

Memory access density (MAD) The ratio of DASD I/Os to the nominal main storage megabytes.

Mode The value that occurs most often in a set of measurements.

Model As used in this book, a model is a mathematical representation of the relationship between two or more variables.

Moderately stochastic As applied to forecasting, the basic causal relationships are known, but data are often incomplete or not available; thus, there is parametric uncertainty in defining the relationships.

Moving average (MA) A time-series method in which the mean of the data for the previous n forecast intervals is used as the forecast for the next interval.

Multidomain Facility An operating system technique, provided by Amdahl Corporation, which allows multiple MVS systems to share the same computer system (with some limitations).

Multiple linear regression Regression analysis in which there are two or more independent (X) variables. Also called multivariate regression.

Multiplicative seasonality A trend-seasonal pattern in which the magnitude of the seasonal fluctuations depends on the level of the data.

Multivariate model Any mathematical model that involves more than two variables.

Natural unit billing A chargeback methodology in which the natural units of the business are used for cost recovery of computer services—for example, charging the customer on the basis of reports, accounts processed, paychecks processed, etc., rather than CPU time, tape mounts, disk space, etc.

Natural unit forecasting A forecasting technique that uses causal models. The predictor variable(s) is taken from the units that describe business activity rather than from computer metrics.

Nominal capacity The theoretical capacity that exists in name only, not in actuality.

Normalization A scaling technique used to assess the resource profiles of multiple workloads running on computers with different capacities. Normalization permits comparisons relative to some common scale. Normalization is typically used in cost accounting and chargeback disciplines where the cost of running a workload can be equalized (despite performance differences such as execution time) across multiple systems (for example, in a shared spool environment where jobs arrive from a central point but may be dispatched on any of several computers or multiple operating system images within the same complex). It may also be used in sizing workloads to determine their "fit" relative to multiple platforms of differing capacities.

Over-initiation In MVS systems, a condition in which the number of concurrent batch address spaces begins to cause performance degradation (less than optimal throughput) due to the system overhead required to manage the workloads.

p value The probability value that a value could result from chance alone.

Parameter As used in information systems the term refers to a numeric value, such as a constant or a coefficient. Managers who are not inclined to mathematical thinking may use the term to refer to the condition of something, such as "the parameters of a situation." Strictly speaking, in statistical terms, parameters always refer to population characteristics (as compared to sample characteristics, which are called "statistics").

Parametric As used in information systems, this usually means the specification of automatic processes by the use of keywords or symbols (macros and related) as compared to programming the processes themselves (which is considered "algorithmic").

Pend time In MVS systems, refers to I/O delay caused when no path or director is available for the DASD device, when the device is engaged in I/O for another channel subsystem or when the device is reserved for exclusive use by another system.

Performance management Performance management is the process of planning, defining, measuring, analyzing, reporting, and tuning the performance of information system resources, including networks, hardware, operating systems, applications, and services. The objective of performance management is the effective application of procedures that optimize the use of systems resources while achieving committed user service levels.

Performance objectives Relative to service-level administration, the areas of attainment of the service-level agreement, such as dependability of service, availability, etc.

Peripheral devices An ancient term from the time when any device other than the expensive CPU was considered "peripheral." Usually refers to data storage devices such as disk and tape.

Platforms The physical resources of a computer system.

Point forecast A forecast consisting of a single number, as opposed to an interval forecast, which is a range of values within which the true value is expected to fall.

Practical capacity The maximum use that can be processed on a particular resource at an acceptable level of performance.

Prediction interval In strict mathematical terminology, the confidence limit, when used in linear regression, is called the *prediction interval.*

Prediction-realization diagram A scattergram that shows the relationship between forecast values and actual values. It is used to determine visually how well a forecasting method is performing.

Predictor variable An explanatory variable or independent variable. It predicts the result of the dependent variable in regression modeling.

Principal-component analysis A statistical analysis, which allows finding the weights (the principal factors) that provide the maximum discrimination among the components.

Process density of memory resident data (PDM) PDM represents the processing cost (per second) that is associated with having on-line 1 megabyte of nominal main storage capacity.

Productivity metrics Throughput as the number of requests per unit of time. These are data that deal with the number of items, such as queue length, number of MVS initiators, or number of VMS processes. Also included in this category are data that deal with rate (occurrences of something per unit of time).

Quadratic model A model with a squared term (second-degree) in it. The trend line for such a model is parabolic.

Quantitative Objective; mathematical. A general approach to the interpretation of data with no implications regarding the validity of the results.

Quantitative forecasting Forecasting that makes use of mathematical models.

Queuing model A "waiting line" model. The name derives from the study of "queues," for example, when people are waiting in line for service at a grocery store. These types of models are often used by performance analysts to predict the results of system behavior, given a specified set of conditions.

R or r   See *Correlation Coefficient.*

R^2 or R squared   See *Coefficient Of Determination.*

Random   Unpredictable. When applied to a series of data, this term means that any value within a specified range has an equal probability of being the next one to occur in the series. When applied to error in a regression model, it means error that could not be predicted by the model.

Reaction time   The interval between the time a job or process is submitted and the beginning of its execution.

Recursive model   A mathematical model that utilizes a series of repetitive calculations, each of which depends upon the result of the previous repetition. For example, weighted linear regression is a recursive model because it builds on the results of previous calculations over a specified range of times.

Regression coefficient   In a regression model, the beta or *b* value, which represents the slope of the line.

Relative I/O content (R)   R is the workload's propensity to generate disk I/O operations as the relevant code is being processed. The disk I/O rate and the CPU busy, when measured for a recurring workload of a system image over sustained periods of time (usually a period of one to three weeks during which no major change in workload composition or supporting software occurs), are in a more or less constant ratio relative to a measure of processor throughput capacity.

Residuals   In regression, the distances between the regression line and the actual data values; i.e., the residuals are the differences between the forecast values and the actual values, so they tell you how much of the variation in the data is not explained by the regression model.

Resource accounting   Chargeback. Analyzing the cost of MIS and billing this cost to the consumers of MIS resources.

Resource categorization   The categorization of system resources into physical, abstract, virtual, or logical.

Resource exhaustion   The end of a resource capacity.

Response metrics Refers to those measurements that represent the time between arrival of a request for service and its delivery. These are data that deal with duration, such as response time or turnaround time.

Response time The time between arrival of a request for service and its delivery is the response time.

Response variable Another name for the dependent or outcome (Y) variable in a regression model.

Robust In mathematical terminology, this implies that the statistic is reliable, regardless of the distribution of the data values.

Rotational delay This is the time required to orient a disk drive over the position requested. In MVS I/O subsystems, the disk is not connected to the channel or storage director during rotational delay, thus leaving them free to start, or complete, I/O operations for other devices.

SAR Abbreviation for Seasonal Autoregressive.

SARIMA Abbreviation for Seasonal Autoregressive Integrated Moving Average.

Scatter diagram A two-dimensional graph showing individual data points. It is often used to show the relationship between two variables (see *Correlation*). A useful first step in analyzing many kinds of data. Also called scatter graph, scatter plot, or scattergram.

Scenario An imaginary future situation. Used in judgmental forecasting.

Scratch An output tape. A tape that is "blank" or made blank by "scratching" the tape (referring to the act of removing previous tape data).

Seasonal autoregressive (SAR) model A time-series model.

Seasonal data A pattern of data values that varies significantly and consistently from one season to another.

Seek delay In MVS I/O subsystems, this refers to the time required for positioning of the read/write head (for DASD) on the cylinder requested (assuming it is different from the prior request). The average seek time for 3380 type devices is approximately 5 milliseconds.

Serialization The arrangement of computer workloads in such a way that they are queued to run one at a time.

Server holding time   The amount of time a computer server is busy servicing a task.

Service charges   Service charges determine the price of the service to be used for customer billing (associated with natural units) and, without predetermined natural units, which are cost sensitive, the price may be the cost (for internal customers) or the cost plus some profit margin (for external customers, or if MIS is a "profit center").

Service-level administration   Management of the speed, accuracy, and availability of MIS services. A systems management control discipline, which is focused on the attainment of a contract for systems operations services, or a service-level agreement.

Service-level agreement   A written agreement, which defines the levels of service to be provided by the information systems environment and includes the methods to measure, control, report, and manage information systems.

Service-level capacity   What the system is capable of providing in terms of *service.*

Service-level deliverables   Those activities, products, or results that MIS provides to the enterprise. The quantification of MIS service is called a service level.

Service-level management   Service-level management is the process of negotiating and defining the levels of service to be provided by the IS environment and includes the methods to measure, control, report, and manage IS systems. The objective is for the information systems environment and the receiver of services to understand service-level requirements, balance them against affordability, reach agreement on how those requirements will be fulfilled, and establish a documented agreement (the service-level agreement).

Service-level objectives   Service-level objectives are service goals that are formal, documented, and recognized in some official way throughout MIS. The customers may, or may not, be aware of these objectives. They are used to approach the problem of organizational control from the standpoint of system coordination, integration, and operation.

Service-level targets These are the measures of good service. In essence they represent the bounds within service that are recognized to be acceptable, identify what services require attention (e.g., tuning, renegotiation of agreements, upgrades, additional resources, etc.), and indicate when enough attention has been accomplished.

Service levels Service levels are categories of measurable system behavior, which are highly correlated to the service objectives of the MIS organization. Each system provides a set of services. Knowledge of the services and outcomes is important in selecting the right metrics and workloads for *service-level administration*.

Significance A statistical judgment based on a confidence level, which means that at the *n* percent confidence level, *n* out of 100 times a similar result would not have been obtained by chance alone.

Simulation A trial run of a mathematical model, using some method of approximating a real-life situation.

Spectral analysis A data analysis technique, which is based on the frequency with which certain outcomes are observed.

Standard deviation A statistic commonly used as a measure of dispersion. Also, approximately equivalent to the square root of the variance.

Standard offerings These identify the services of MIS that are included as part of all service-level agreements. They include customer support activities, such as records management (production control and migration, scheduled maintenance, emergency maintenance, restart and recovery, disaster recovery), security, and other considerations (system problems, i.e., hardware, system software, and communication/network outages).

Stepwise regression A multiple regression technique in which the analysis places the independent variables into the model one at a time, beginning with the one that has the most explanatory value. Often used to eliminate unnecessary predictor variables.

Storage class One of four groups of parameters that describe data to a systems-managed storage environment. With storage class parameters, a storage administrator can specify data set service levels in terms of millisecond response times.

Storage group   One of four groups of parameters used to describe data requirements for a systems-managed storage environment. Storage groups are specific disks with similar performance thresholds that are available for different kinds of data sets. The concept of storage groups should be familiar to most administrators already working with disk pools.

Strategic reserves   Extra or unused capacity of a system, which can be brought to bear on conditions of unprecedented demand for resources. Resources are reserved, i.e., planned surplus capacity, for the specific purpose of meeting demand that is expected but uncertain.

Systems-managed storage (SMS)   A disk management concept based on share and guide user recommendations of the late 1970s and early 1980s. IBM's implementation of SMS is a series of software products first released in the late 1980s. The general idea of SMS is to feed desired system parameters, such as maximum response time, into the system and, based on parameters, data set names, and other criteria, have the system select appropriate, non-volume-specific disks to hold the data.

Systems management controls   A body of techniques and procedures to plan, organize, operate, measure, and control information systems. In order to accomplish these objectives, IS management has evolved disciplines that form a framework for effective systems management. These management disciplines are focused on the control of systems in order to meet business goals.

TCB time   Task Control Block time. In MVS, the time spent specifically running the application program, as compared to SRB (System Request Block) time, during which the application program is waiting for a system-level event.

Technological forecasting   A judgmental forecasting method based on considerations of trends in technology. In capacity planning, long-term projections of resource requirements are often combined with expectations about future technology regarding resource capacity, footprint, etc., of the future computer systems.

Theoretical capacity   The capacity of a resource based on the theoretical behavior or geometry. Typically, the actual capacity is less than the theoretical capacity due to system software overhead, patterns of use, etc.

Throughput   Throughput is the rate at which the requests of the system can be serviced.

Time horizon   The length of time in the future for which the forecast is prepared. In capacity planning, the time horizon is usually no further into the future than the length of time for which data are available from the past.

Time-series analysis   Any mathematical method for analyzing a series of data points collected at uniform intervals over time.

Tracking signal   A procedure for monitoring forecasts by determining whether they are consistently higher or lower than actual values. If so, then a tracking signal trip results, which notifies the forecaster.

Trend   The long-term tendency of a series of data values, usually of a time series. In business, usually means a "straight line" trend.

Trend analysis   A form of linear regression in which time is the independent variable. A form of time-series analysis. The best way of drawing a straight line since the invention of the straight edge.

Trending data   Time-series data that show a statistically significant pattern of change over time.

Trip   A kind of alarm for "catching" bad forecasts and alerting the analyst to the problem. Just as a burglar might trip an alarm system, a statistical trip sounds the alarm in a similar sense.

Turnaround time   For the batch (noninteractive) environment, *turnaround time* is the interval between the submission of a batch job (IBM) or process (DEC) and its completion (this includes the time to read and process data).

Turning point   A point where the trend changes direction.

Univariate regression   A regression model in which there is one independent (X) variable and one dependent (Y) variable.

Utilization law   A mathematical description, which states that utilization is the product of throughput times the mean service time. The utilization law has the advantage that no assumptions need to be made about variable distribution or interarrival time.

Utilization metrics   Utilization metrics are measures of the percent of time a resource is busy or in use for a given load level.

Variable   A symbol that represents some value of interest.

Variance   This is a measure of the amount of variation in the data. As used in capacity planning, it can represent any kind of difference or variation.

Virtual resource   A virtual resource usually refers to the range of addressable storage encompassing the architecturally defined maximum of the computer system. In MVS systems, this would be an *address space*, in DEC/VAX systems, it would be an *image*. The operating system enables the address space description and the activation of programs within the virtual storage. The objects referenced by application programs are, in effect, translations or mappings from real objects to their virtual counterparts. The virtual objects and their composite structures define the *logical* resources of the system. In virtual storage systems, even data— the fundamental unit of data management being a file or data set—correspond to virtual objects such as *data set control blocks* (MVS).

Wait-time-to-initiate (WTTI)   In MVS systems, this is time a job may be queued to run before it actually starts running. Wait times will be experienced if all available initiators of that class are inactive, drained, or busy. Wait times will also be experienced if there are no initiators of that class.

Weight   The relative importance assigned to one of several variables in a model or to one of several successive values of the same variable. Usually it is expressed as a multiplier.

Weighted average   An average calculated from weighted data, so that some data values have more "influence" than others.

Weighted linear regression   A regression model calculated from weighted data, so that some of the data values influence the result more than others.

Winters method   A method of exponential smoothing designed to accommodate seasonal and trend patterns.

Workload A workload may be described as a list of service requests to the system or, from a modeling point of view, as the probability of various requests. For simulation modeling, a workload may be described as a trace of requests measured on a real system. For business element forecasting and cost analysis, a workload may be described as activity of the system associated with a specific application (or in support of that application), including such abstract entities as subsystems, multiuser single address spaces, batch, interactive processes, or some combination of these that define the application system boundaries.

Workload benchmarking A measurement technique used to determine which hardware configuration best meets a fixed data processing load.

Workload characterization Ideally, the clustering of system activities in statistically useful ways which exploit the natural patterns of resource usage by the system. One may also use volume of work, resource profiles, scheduling information, business function, or combinations of these to define a workload.

Workload identification Same as workload characterization.

Workload parameter The average behavior of each workload component is characterized for modeling purposes by *workload parameters*. Examples include transaction types, paging activity, I/O service requests, etc. The parameters, which depend on the workload, and not the system, are the salient components of the model.

X11 Time-series analysis methods developed by the Bureau of the Census based on the decomposition technique.

Index